BUSINESS WISE GUIDE

BUSINESS WISE GUIDE

80 Powerful Insights
You Can't Learn in Business School

by
MARK O. HUBBARD

BUSINESS WISE GUIDE
80 Powerful Insights
You Can't Learn in Business School

Copyright © 2008 by Mark O. Hubbard

10 9 8 7 6 5 4 3 2 1

ISBN 978-0-9780977-6-9

Published by Corby Books
a division of Corby Publishing
P.O. Box 93
Notre Dame, IN 46556
phone: 574-784-3482
fax: 574-968-7600
email: corbybooks1@aol.com
website: corbypublishing.com

Cover Design by: Trent Gillaspie

Printed in the United States of America

To Bridget, Matt and Nancy,
who have provided me with more good fortune
than a person deserves in one lifetime.

TABLE OF CONTENTS

PREFACE

First, thank you for reading this book. Double the thanks if you purchased the book or passed it along to a friend to read. I'm very serious. You will find as you read **Business Wise Guide** that I sincerely believe in doing the simple, logical and straightforward actions in business that have real impact and meaning. Saying "thank you" is one of those. In fact, you'll find an entire chapter on the subject.

It was never my intention to write a book. The process just appeared too hard. And what could I possibly write that anyone else would want to read? When you discover how few books actually sell over a thousand copies (fewer than 5%) and how little authors actually earn for all their effort (about 10% of the retail price), you wonder if this is a good use of one's time? So, why did I do it? The truth is that this book practically wrote itself. I'm sure that many of you reading this could have done the same thing. I'd encourage you to try. All you need is a good premise and a willingness to tell your story. Here is my story.

Ever since leaving business school in 1975, I've been writing down insights on scraps of paper that I've read, observed or learned. For years, I've been tossing these into a file folder. I've embraced many of these stories and sayings as my own to share with friends, colleagues and clients. The adages tend to slide into my conversations at opportune moments. So much so, that many colleagues now expect that I'll have a "saying" to cover almost every business situation. Friends have been urging me to write down all these "Hubbardisms" in one place. Finally, I decided to do just that. My original intention was to write them for my son as something to leave behind for his future use. Then I started sending my clients individual subject-essays attached to e-mail correspondence. A publisher eventually heard about my personal project and encouraged me to prepare this collection of chapters for a wider audience.

Right up front, I want to dispel any notion that I view myself as an expert in the art of conducting business. Far from it. I've literally made every mistake in the book. I'm like many of you reading this: a keen observer of things in the course of my career. *The point of view I'm taking is that obvious lessons, common sense adages if you will, aren't always so common in business practice.* So, for years, I've been writing down these adages in the hope of trying to improve my own performance and to avoid some of the potholes that seem obvious to an independent observer. This is the point. Things that seem so obvious in the abstract or when they are happening to someone else become confused and garbled when they are part of our own life challenges. Because common sense gets compromised in the heat of the moment, it might be valuable to review it on a regular basis without that stress. That's where **Business Wise Guide** fills a void.

Here's what you can expect. First, I doubt that anything I've written will strike you as either unbelievably or unassailably brilliant. In fact, I'm guessing that almost all of the content of this book will resonate with situations you've already faced in business or in your broader life experiences. I hope that you find the value to this book to be that you now have a simple and entertaining read, a handbook if you will, that reminds you of the things you already know. Then your behavior can start to more closely align with your own accumulated knowledge.

Second, the subtitle of the book is not meant to disparage or undermine the value of a formal business education from one of our finer institutions of higher learning. Proudly, I teach at a couple of them: Rensselaer Polytechnic Institute and the University of Notre Dame. When I entered the MBA program at the Wharton School as a student I had been trained as an architect. I arrived with absolutely zero business knowledge or savvy. For me, every day there was an intense experience - from learning about accounting and statistics to the dreaded (but worthwhile) courses in economics. It was a time of enlightenment that I feel very fortunate to have had. I'd encourage anyone thinking about business school to forge ahead. Your time will be well spent. One book, or an entire library of them, can never be a substitute for that experience.

But, I'll never forget my first employer after business school, Jack LeFort, taking me aside one day with the following conversation. "Mark, I know that you've spent the last two years and lots of money learning things at Wharton. Now, I'm going to tell you the most important thing you'll ever learn in business. I'm guessing that nobody at Wharton ever told you this." At this point I was incredulous, doubting, and waiting for the promised nugget to drop. When it did, I knew he was right (this is the subject of Chapter 1). Jack's piece of wisdom has been invaluable to me. It wasn't something I ever learned in business school. That wasn't because my education was lacking or my professors weren't well prepared. It was simply because what Jack told me was something I couldn't have ever learned in school with the proper appreciation to absorb it. It had to be learned through real world experience, out where they use "live ammo." This book is filled with that kind of street knowledge.

An important thing I want every reader to know is that I don't take personal credit for crafting any of the adages on my own. I've just collected and edited the "headlines" over many years as an observer and a student. Where I can remember a source, I've included it. Even if it came from something I once read, I've tried to be accurate in attribution. Many of the concepts in the book have been talked about for generations. So, this has been akin to writing down an "oral history of business adages." Honestly, it would be impossible to provide original source attribution in most cases. Just to reiterate, I claim none of them as my own. The individual subject areas are all worthy of their own dedicated book.

They probably have already been dissected by scholars and writers much more learned than I. I'd encourage you to dig deeper into more and better material about a particular subject that interests you.

You can read this book in a very short time just by scanning the chapter headings you like. I have a mental picture of you sitting at a comfortable bookstore reading the book for free. That's OK, because maybe then you'll want to buy it and keep it for future reference. Then you can take longer to select those chapter headings that interest you and read them in detail, making your own notes as you do. Or, you can digest the entire text start to finish. This would be a good approach for sitting in an airline seat, hopefully in First Class. My goal is for the content to be readable, memorable and usable. The first time you verbally share one of these adages with a colleague, I've achieved my goal.

However you use ***Business Wise Guide,*** I encourage you to write liberally over the pages and margins with you own thoughts and insights. Used to its fullest extent, this book might serve as an interesting point of departure for leaders and management teams to literally "get on the same page." If every reader utilizes just one insight I'll consider my time and effort well worth it. I'll also consider the price of this book to be an excellent value. I'm passionate about adding value.

A book of this kind really isn't finished and never should be. I already have more observations recorded and new chapters formatted than would fit into a reasonably-sized second edition. I'm hoping that readers, like you, will provide me with even more material so that the sequel will also write itself. To assist in this process I've reserved the web address, www. BusinessWiseGuide.net. I'd welcome your thoughts and insights. We all still have a lot to learn.

SECTION I
MONEY WISE

You make money
when you buy
(not when you sell)

This is the piece of wisdom that was imparted by my first employer after business school, Jack LeFort, which I referenced in the Preface. Imagine my skepticism in 1975, when Jack told me that he was about to share the most important business lesson he knew, and it was something I probably hadn't learned at the Wharton School, where he was once a student himself. It turns out he was correct on both counts. I didn't learn this in business school. And it has been the single most important piece of business guidance I've ever received.

So, let's put this into context, lest you think I spent all of my time in school with my head in a sack. This is *not* the same as the old saw to "buy low and sell high." At least that's not it exactly. Generations of business students and leaders have been repeating that adage. The spread between the buying price and the selling price is profit – and practically everything we do in business school, and beyond, has a profit motive. Or, at least we should be adding value.

No, the subtlety to this is that the money you make (if any), or the value added, is almost always established at the point of buying something that you will eventually sell. Sure, you realize the gain from an accounting viewpoint at the time of the sale. But that isn't when you actually make the money. It doesn't matter if you buy something as a whole or as component parts. It also doesn't matter if the original goods or services are sold or if they are retooled or enhanced in some fashion. *The simple advice is that you must work very hard to buy things right.*

This also acknowledges a simple, but conveniently ignored truth in business: the selling price of a good or service is very rarely determined unilaterally by the seller. In fact, selling prices are almost always market driven. For unique or scarce items they are determined by the buyer's level of interest or need.

When you sell something, you are hoping for either an uninformed buyer (usually a matter of degree) or a highly motivated buyer to maximize the selling price. That is a good thing if and when it happens. But, why depend on that happening as a matter of chance? Better to depend on your own knowledge and cunning when you buy something, so that you have a higher probability of eventually selling at a profit. Therefore, acknowledge that you will actually make the money you will eventually reap, not at the moment of sale, but at the moment of your initial purchase(s).

Of course, this guidance can be applied to almost any purchase in business, and life. You make money when you efficiently buy and employ human resources. You make money when you effectively buy technology and cost-saving techniques. You make money when you spend the lowest possible price for commodities. In fact, it could be said that when you stop thinking in this manner, you are probably well on your way to stopping the process of making money.

The adage of "making money when you buy" is profound. That's because it is a fundamental truth, and because embracing it can change your behavior for a lifetime. It is something I've used practically every day in my business and personal life, from buying real estate, to buying stocks, to buying office equipment to buying used cars (I never buy new). When I challenge myself to find the lowest cost for purchasing something (holding quality constant), I'm almost always surprised to find that I can buy things much cheaper than I originally thought, or lower than the price originally asked for by the seller. All these savings go directly into my pocket immediately – even if it takes time to cash them in.

Looking back on my formal education, I'm quite surprised that there weren't courses taught in how to buy things properly and efficiently (just as surprising is that there aren't courses in selling things either). I'm still involved with business schools, teaching as an adjunct professor, and I still don't see much in formal education around the subjects of purchasing and negotiating. I don't know if it is because the subjects are inherently "non-academic" or it is because academics don't have to embrace the realities of day-to-day business practice. Whatever the reason, buying right is a classic example of something you can't actually learn in business school.

If you only read and absorb one chapter of this book, this was the one to sample. The lesson here is something that has so many applications to issues that face the CEO, the manager and every business person, almost every day. In fact, it applies to every aspect of financially managing your life.

2

ALL MONEY HAS PERSONALITY

This is a lesson I learned by working alongside Frank Osborn in the late 1980's when he was starting up a public radio company and I was the COO. I've never heard anyone else even think in terms of money having a personality. But, I believe it does. And, I'm not referring here to the personalities of George Washington, Abraham Lincoln, Thomas Jefferson or the other dead Presidents that are pictured on United States currency.

The background for this observation encompasses a number of decades of being engaged in the process of developing new, start-up businesses and improving established ones. There is invariably a point in the growth process where new or additional capital is needed to acquire, re-structure or re-energize a business or venture. This is when the personalities behind all the money (old and new), the people and institutions actually providing the funds and using the funds, start to have very distinctive qualities.

It is easy to predict what the entrepreneurs behind a new or on-going business have on their minds. They believe that without their initial idea, or the months and years of their laborious struggling, the business wouldn't be in the attractive spot of needing additional money for growth. Predictably, they overestimate the value of their idea. Elsewhere in this book we point out that ideas are either priceless or worthless. When you need additional capital, ideas are caught somewhere in between but certainly not yet leaning toward priceless. So, the party looking for money always overestimates the fair market value of their contribution up until the point where the money is needed. The approach they take in negotiating for funds is a reflection of their own perception of their position on the game board, along with their own personality quirks as individuals.

The folks providing the potential money can be more complicated. They generally start from a foundation of trying to understand the risk and return equation for their money were they to invest. This sounds pretty academic and straightforward. In practice it rarely is. This is because each party supplying money has a distinct risk profile, a time horizon, a control proclivity, along with many obvious (and some not so obvious) prejudices. They may have a low tolerance for risk and need to structure a guarantee that their money will be returned. Or, they may be less risk sensitive because they have the background and confidence to believe that they have a higher understanding of a business or industry and therefore can force positive changes. Investors have an almost unlimited number of choices, so they can be picky. Here again, the personality of the money is very much the personality of the individual investor(s).

One trend is universally predicable in the funding process. The people responsible for investing money employ excruciatingly detailed analysis to understand risk and to mitigate as much of it as possible for enhanced returns. On a scale from absolute uncertainty (the raw idea) to absolute certainty (when the business is sold and the check clears), the progressive categories are: risk recognition, risk understanding, risk management and risk control. Each of these generates different personality expressions from the sources of risk capital, be they individuals or institutions.

Understanding "money personality" is of critical importance for a couple of reasons. First, a business may never get the funding it needs without a complete understanding of the personalities of the money being solicited and then the necessary goal of raising capital is thwarted. Related to this, by not "zoning in" on the likely personalities (behind the money) of interested investors, a stressful process becomes more frustrating and time consuming.

Second, and perhaps more importantly, *the personality of the money you get on "day one" of the investment cycle usually doesn't change for the better over time.* In fact, almost all investors with significant stakes will become progressively more engaged with the business once their money is in play. Sometimes this is very beneficial to the management team and the enterprise. But this often leads to inevitable conflicts. When a business doesn't perform as first advertised, the personalities of all parties get strained and distorted, usually in a fashion that is counterproductive to solving the problems at hand.

It is very much like a marriage. Be careful who you marry in business. You will have to live with your partner's idiosyncrasies for a long time. The alternative is a messy and a costly divorce. In the end, the personality of the money always has more clout than the founder's or management because deals are structured to insure this. So, for a CEO it is essential for survival to understand the personalities of all the money in play.

For reasons relating to a lower cost of capital, companies often take the route of issuing public shares when they can. Debt (with an interest component) may be converted to equity which is less burdensome. The associated benefit is that a large, dispersed group of stakeholders may be easier for the company to manage. One-on-one accountability is diluted (or non-existent) for practical purposes. This might work for a while. But, eventually the personality of this category of dispersed money will also emerge. A class of shareholders may become active and then you are subject to the (usually not-so-lovable) personality of their legal counsel. Or worse yet, there could be official government intervention (SEC, FTC, etc.) and their pit bull personalities will make the security lawyers seem like golden retrievers.

This is a lesson that most of us learn early in life when we need money from our parents. There are always strings attached. Real life is even more demanding. When you need someone else's money, just remember that the money comes with a personality. Is it one you like? And/or, is it one you can live with?

3

REMEMBER THE
MONEY VALUE OF TIME

Anyone who has ever been to business school re-
calls being drilled from practically the first day with
the "time value of money" concept. Exercises are con-
structed to emphasize the "net present value" of a series
of projected cash flows as a tool to make informed decisions today about future events. It is a necessary thing
to learn and once in a while, it proves to be useful in
actual business practice.

The problem is that in real life a projected stream of
cash flows is anything but predictable. This very fact
places all the accuracy of mathematics on the fringe of
actually being useless in common practice. Risks are
all built into the assumptions. Calculating the probabilities of business variables should clarify the analysis and
assist you in making a more informed decision. But,
after you look out more than a couple of years the mix of
permutations and combinations becomes vast and overwhelming. In pursuit of simplicity, sometimes there is
a reversion to simple formulas and best estimates for
future outcomes. It all sounds reasonable, and it is – in
theory. It is also very dangerous.

What I'm suggesting in this chapter is that there is another way to look at outcomes and the future. And, along the way, I'm challenging you to consider whether or not an investment, or a reinvestment, in a business or enterprise actually makes the most sense. To do this, challenge yourself with an alternative based on simple math and patience.

The backside of the "time value of money" concept is my "money value of time" concept. Consider this. It wouldn't take a financial genius to get 5-8% compounded in a nearly risk-free market instrument over a long time horizon. What does this mean? Well, using the inverse of the "Rule of 70" (some use the "Rule of 72," but for practical purposes they are the same), it would mean that an investment would double somewhere between nine (70 divided by 8) and fourteen (70 divided by 5) years. There are some prominent Fortune 500 companies that actually have doubled shareholder value every five years over long stretches of time. But, it isn't a trivial accomplishment.

So, let's agree, there are painless alternatives to making high risk investments in your own ideas or in your internal organization which ultimately could provide superior returns. This is what informed investors do – maximize their returns. Putting yourself into the investor frame of mind may change the entire equation before you blindly forge ahead. Using internal funds to invest in a project with almost no chance of success is just plain stupid against this benchmark. You can get richer on the slower and safer road.

It isn't inconsequential to think in these terms. When it relates to our personal investment portfolios, we should be doing this all the time. One of my professors at the Wharton School, Scott Armstrong, walked into class one day and asked for a show of hands. How many in the class aspired to be millionaires someday? This was back in 1973, when $1 million had a lot more spending power. After every hand was raised, he went to the backboard (this was before white boards) and did some calculations to demonstrate how much would have to be saved each year from the ages of 25 to 65 to have $1 million at retirement. The annual savings number didn't seem that large and the imputed growth rate was quite low at the time. We've all seen other calculations along the same line. How much you would need to save every year for the first ten years of a person's life in order to pay for college at age seventeen (with some imputed inflation)? Again, the number isn't as large as you might imagine.

I actually employed some of this thinking myself. I wouldn't want to be accused of not eating the food out of my own advice kitchen. I was able to sock-away some decent bonus checks for my son's education when he was between three and eight (for a total of about $25,000). When he actually went to college at age eighteen, and thanks to a robust stock market, he had about $180 thousand in his account. The market continued to flourish for a couple more years when he was a student. After paying all his room, board, tuition and fees (at Notre Dame) he still had $60 thousand left. We finally finished draining this account during his last year of medical school (at a private university, with tuition over $40 thousand per year). Yes, we supplemented his expenses in small ways. But the heavy lifting was done by the money we saved when he was a very young boy.

Taking this same approach to a business, imagine if companies saved half of their retained earnings to be invested wisely in index funds. Then they reinvested the other half on internal projects. More than a few companies would have performed magnificently under this theory because they would have been forced to invest less in very high-risk internal projects which never had a chance of delivering shareholder value.

So, considering the "money value of time" could have whopping implications for the value of a company, or your personal portfolio. Simple math, time and patience are the defining ingredients.

4

THE POWER OF A DOUBLE

There is an unwritten rule in expected executive behavior. Business results should at least double every five years. This rule is generally ignored, usually through arrogance or ignorance. However, it is like gravity. It is always there and it is a powerful force. Moreover, not paying attention to the rule is done at one's own peril.

When resources are applied and management is competent, results should double naturally in five years. If things don't double in about five years, there is the tendency to question whether or not management is competent, independent of whether or not sufficient resources were dedicated to the venture. This is a simple concept – profound and accurate.

So, what "things" are supposed to double every five years? For starters, things like operating profit, or market share, or earnings, or share price. These are all frequently used benchmarks that become scorecards for CEOs. On the flip side, there are definitely things that shouldn't double – like debt, or size of staff, or number of complaints, or stock analysts providing negative reports.

The prevailing sentiment is that any executive worth his or her salt should be able to make things happen, build the business and add value. In the absence of tangible evidence that an executive is squarely on track to double a business unit's metrics, a search should be conducted to find someone who can. Right or wrong, this is the underlying thinking driving for-profit enterprises. From the view point of shareholders, it is completely reasonable. This is because a complete idiot can usually find a place to invest money that will double in seven to ten years without looking very hard and with practically no risk at all. Surely, an ongoing business run by smart people should do better and provide higher rewards for slightly higher risk.

One of the consequences of this unwritten rule is that upwardly mobile executives must place themselves in positions to win – to create the double. Taking on impossible tasks may seem like worthy challenges, especially when your boss makes a fuss about you being the most qualified person to achieve success. Sometimes tough tasks are the fast lane to actually creating a double. With a little tinkering and some expense reduction, doubling the bottom line may be accomplished quickly. These are assignments to seek out, take on and embrace. But when a business is stuck in "the mud" and many attempts to solve a particular problem haven't been successful, chances are this isn't a good situation for a double. Then there are some organizations that are just too big to ever see a double in five years. This happens because there is a "base period" number that is mathematically too large. How can you double the revenues or the profits at GE every five years, for example?

The power of doubling the size and profitability of an organization is amazing. How do certain people always seem to be in the right place to take advantage of these opportunities? It's because they are always looking for these situations, either by design or instinct. They swing at the pitches that in the strike zone. Then, they also have the skills to deliver in a timely fashion. There isn't an executive or a gambler who is consistently lucky. But you can be consistently smart. Learn to embrace the rules of doubling and you might be amazed at your career progress and success.

I recall an interesting corollary factoid from a television show *(Numbers)*. Take a piece of paper and fold it in half. Then refold the remaining piece over on itself. It turns out that if you were able to physically do that fifty (50) times (just folding the paper over on itself) you would reach the Sun. This seems too fantastic to believe. I shared this premise with a first-year MBA class at Rensselaer Polytechnic Institute. There are many gifted engineering and math types attending this well-known and respected school. While many in the audience were shaking their heads, one fellow yelled out from the back of the room in a surprised voice: "He's right!" (Consider the math - one hundredth of an inch to the fiftieth power.) The lesson is that the first couple of folds, or doubles, are the easiest. That fiftieth one is pretty big – in fact, it starts half way to the Sun.

The financial equivalent of the dramatic example above is to start working for a penny on "day one" and then double the daily wage every day for a month. At the end of 30 days the process would yield a combined earned sum of \$5,304,000. Go for five additional days and the sum grows to \$339,456,652. The point is that even if you start small the compounded results of doubling become quite large after multiple cycles.

Time is not your career's friend. So, find situations where doubles are possible in fewer than five years and then deliver the goods. Your career will advance with surprising velocity.

5

HAVE CASH WHEN
NOBODY ELSE HAS CASH

This is a very valuable piece of advice from an unlikely business source, but a very well-known person for other historic accomplishments.

I had the pleasure of doing some consulting projects for the Johnson Family when they owned radio stations in Austin, Texas (having already sold their television properties). At the time, the stations were owned jointly by former First Lady, Lady Bird Johnson and her daughter, Lucy Baines Johnson Turpin. Day-to-day, I worked directly with Lucy and her husband. But I did have occasion to meet with the former First Lady at private dinners in the course of the assignment. She was as astute a business person as I've ever met – although she was in her early 80's at the time. I was totally impressed and charmed by Mrs. Johnson and value the friendship she extended to me.

Over one dinner conversation I asked her, "How did you get involved in broadcasting and make so much money?" I think this was a story she enjoyed telling and it went something like this.

Claudia (her given name) Johnson inherited a modest but meaningful sum of money when her father died in the 1940's. Like so many of us, she was perplexed by how to invest wisely. But, she knew that she did want to invest it, as opposed to spending it. (As I mentioned, this was an instinctively sharp lady.) So, she went to a friend of her father's, "Judge" Roy Hofienz – who later was famous for developing the Astrodome in Houston, billed at the time (1969) as the "Eighth Wonder of the World." Essentially, she asked the judge the same question that I asked her, "How did you make your money?"

As she related the story, the judge leaned over his desk, adjusted his glasses, and then gave her this advice: "I've learned that it is important to have cash when nobody else has cash." That's it. All in one sentence.

So, she took the judge's advice. She held on to her money (her dry powder). She waited for a good opportunity to come along that was priced right, because nobody else wanted to, or could, do a cash transaction. In the late 1940's, this opportunity came in broadcasting, specifically in television which at the time was perceived as an expensive industry to enter with a speculative and unproven business model. Now, it didn't hurt that her husband was well-connected in both Texas and Washington and could smooth the path for her at the FCC.

But it was all her money. And, essentially she followed the judge's advice. This is a story that I treasure from a wonderful person I was privileged to know. Now, I'm sharing the treasure with you.

6

Don't trust anyone else to invest your money

At first, this may sound like a pretty draconian position to take. Never mind that it may also be somewhat unrealistic. But, I think there are compelling reasons for executives to be personally involved with all the investment decisions that are made in their names, both professionally and personally. So, it's not about letting other people provide you with advice. It is about trusting them implicitly, with blinders on, that is to be avoided. In fact, it is something that I'd advise you never to do.

Consider the responsibility of investing money, either as a pure job definition (like a mutual fund manager, or even for your own account), or in the form of getting corporate resources committed to a project, or approving expenses to accomplish a company goal or directive. The implication is always that you are being entrusted with a very precious resource – capital. There is ownership, hard work and personality behind all of that capital, because someone had to earn it. There are personal expectations behind the scenes for the deployment of that capital. There is a story behind every single dollar, even if you don't know it. Given that, there are also presumptions (implied, specified or legal) about the process and efficiency you will use once that capital is entrusted to you.

The most important consideration is that someone is always watching (or should be), and not totally trusting you (correctly) to do the right thing. So, why on earth would you break the chain of trust by not taking full responsibility for this precious resource? It can be said that you always have a "fiduciary responsibility" at any level of management. Does the guidance in this chapter make more sense now?

There is an equally compelling reason not to trust anyone else (over and above the fact that nobody probably fully trusts you). What if things go badly with decisions made by people under you? You won't be able to blame them, no matter how much you try. The organizational hierarchy will ask you for an explanation. You will have to step forward and take responsibility for failure. It is better to step in front of this issue and pro- actively avoid failure. Then if something fails, at least it was your fault. Make no mistake about it: you'll be held accountable either way.

On the positive side, you will be missing tremendous learning opportunities if you don't take responsibility for your investments, in business or at home. There are new data points for you to assimilate when your investments are solid and productive. There are equally valuable, however painful or embarrassing, data points when investments don't go well. More often, results fall into the space between "over-the-moon" success and "black-hole" failure. So, as a practical matter there is always something to learn by staying on top of the capital entrusted to you and constant opportunities to make productive adjustments.

Before you think that this advice is totally lopsided, allow me to make a clarification. I'm not suggesting that you shouldn't seek the best possible advice when making business or personal investment decisions. It would be stupid not to do that, plain and simple. So, I would encourage you to seek out and use experienced advisors. Undoubtedly, they will help you make better decisions. Listen to them carefully. Sometimes their best advice is buried in the sub-text of what is said. If you don't understand what they are proposing, ask simple straightforward questions. This may not mean that their answers will emerge as convincing. But, in the process of following this process two things will happen: 1) you will test "their game," and 2) you will put them on notice to sharpen "their game." Be careful who you trust - who will tell you the truth and provide well-considered, enduring advice. Even then, you must make the ultimate decisions.

The most unforgivable business failure is to make the same mistake over and over and over. If other people are spending company resources with your good name and reputation on the line, you must sleep with one eye open. Rest assured someone you are accountable to is doing exactly that when their head hits the pillow.

SECTION II
DEAL WISE

7

YOU CAN'T MAKE A GOOD DEAL WITH A BAD PERSON

I credit this adage to father, Donald Hubbard. He was trained as an engineer, and was a very precise and honest man in all of his dealings. In fact, he was one of those rare individuals who made sure that the other party in a transaction he was involved with would get exactly what was promised or even more. "Under promise and then over deliver" was a part of the man's character.

The premise here is simple. When you are working on a transaction where meaningful money is at stake, "character matters."

My dad would tell me that it was more important to understand the motivations and the character of the people involved in a business deal than to initially focus on the numbers or the viability of the transaction. His thinking was pretty straightforward. If he didn't respect the individuals doing a deal, the terms of the deal really didn't matter much. He just walked away and in so doing probably saved himself significant time and aggravation. I have to say that his adherence to this principle was one of the hallmarks of what people remembered about him after his death in 1990: a man of sterling character. I have found, both in business and in my personal life, his advice has served me well. On the rare occasions when I have ignored his advice, I have been disappointed with the outcomes.

Of course, my dad instinctively knew what all good deal makers know: *the terms of a deal are the reflection of people making the deal.* Many approach a deal with either a "screw the other guy" or a "buyer beware" mindset. They attempt to win every business point by trying to see just how far they can push the other party. Some of this is absolutely fair gamesmanship. But without trust, you really can't ever know for sure if the line has been crossed into unfair or dangerous ground. It doesn't matter what side of the deal you are on, buyer or seller. What you can ascertain is when you are entering into the "twilight zone" because you start to feel the person you are negotiating with has become an untrustworthy "slime ball." It makes the negotiating process uncomfortable, dangerous and practically unproductive, if you really can't trust anything that is said, written or promised.

Likewise, when you are party to a deal, make no mistake that experienced and honest deal makers on the other side are evaluating you. Your good name and reputation mean everything to your ability to consistently conduct business. Another of my dad's adages applies here: "The only thing you can't buy back is your reputation."

As I do work for my clients, I keep looking for the exceptions to Don Hubbard's rules. I have found precious few. I do see regrets. The people making deals can eventually become unhappy with the outcomes. Sometimes it is either buyer's or seller's remorse. Sometimes it is because of their own incompetence, unfounded exuberance or stupidity. Perhaps unexpected market forces take a turn against them. Executives can usually sleep with these outcomes, as bad as they might be, so long as there isn't any lingering guilt that they were "had" in the transaction by an unscrupulous partner. However, knowing in their guts that they didn't trust the other side of a deal turned bad, but still proceeded, is the worst kind of regret I've seen with successful executives. The pain is even worse when the mistake is made again, and then again. This is a special brand of torture that few can tolerate. Eventually they do learn. My father had it right, you can't make a good deal with a bad person.

Alas, some deals actually have bad people negotiating on both sides. The delicious justice here is that probably both sides "get what's coming to them."

8

YOU NEVER RUN OUT OF DEALS

Searching for viable deals is akin to dating. When you finally get your first kiss your brain sends you a signal that it feels really good and maybe you should try again for a second kiss. Searching for new people to date is hard work. There is the tendency to stick with the people that are kissing you, because the hard work is over. Right? So, people stay in relationships and they stay interested in potential deals for some of the same reasons. One of these reasons - they believe that they'll run out of people to date, or run out of deals to do. (This chapter is the companion to Chapter 9. You should read them together for the complete effect.)

When you are in the deal-making process there are times when you hit dry patches. Either the deal flow is light (too many people chasing too few deals turns the flow into a trickle), or you are seeing too many deals, all of questionable merit (as experienced in the so-called ".com bust"). I've witnessed both sides of the spectrum and the large space in between. There is an inherent impatience in the character of deal-makers. So, no matter where you are in the spectrum of opportunity there is the feeling that deals are in short supply. Worse is the mistaken assumption that "all the good deals have been done."

My observation is that this is never the case. Lots of deal flow doesn't necessarily mean more good deals. And small deal flow doesn't mean that all the good deals have been picked-over (although sometimes this temporarily does happen).

The important thing is to know what you are looking for, and then to have the *ability to be decisive* once you find it. I do think it is true that "good deals don't hang around too long." But, there always seem to be enough deals to look at. In the process of looking at all deals you tend to meet new people, some of whom might bring you the next good deal you'll see.

Sometimes it is valuable to inspect a deal just to test your criteria. As a person that also tries to bring new deals to interested investors, I've seen every excuse in the book for not doing a deal. All of them are quite valid. The deal is too small, or too large, or early stage, or not in our domain expertise – the list goes on and on. But, the folks I talk with always seem to have some deal flow. They don't appear desperate or they would be looking harder at all the opportunities that outsiders, like me, present. That said, the saddest case for everyone is when I get called a year after an initial denial with the question: "What ever happened to that company, anyway?" Deal criteria can also be fluid. When pitching a deal, the first "no" may not be final.

In general, don't worry about finding good deals. Maybe they aren't apparent right now. But like New England weather, if you don't like it, all you have to do is wait a minute.

9

LET THE DEALS COME TO YOU

Most of us are engaged in deal-making to some degree, large or small. This chapter is directed toward those people who make deals for a living, buying and selling items of substantial value – like capital equipment or entire companies.

This chapter is not suggesting that the people in the business of deal-making should be passive. No, quite the contrary. I believe that deal-makers should be in the deal flow and always looking for and evaluating new, or better, deals. How else are they going to find ones that might meet their investment objectives? So, keep the wheels in motion and new deals churning at all times.

What I am suggesting is that it is *not in the best interest of a deal-maker to chase a deal.* There are two reasons for this: 1) during the process of chasing a deal you might unknowingly become irrational about the internal fundamentals and possible returns, and 2) chasing deals shades the negotiations in favor of the other party (as either the buyer or the seller, this ultimately costs you money and lowers your eventual return).

There are always deals being offered. In good times (especially) it is difficult to pick up a financial publication and not find some party chasing a deal. Not only is it costly to chase a deal, it is even more costly to chase a deal in public with the financial press watching. This may, in part, explain why some of the largest mergers in history have become some of the biggest busts (Time Warner into AOL comes to mind).

By letting the deal come to you, you gain much useful data which will help in the negotiation process. It should be very advantageous to understand why the seller is selling and what other pressure points might be exploited. It might be interesting to know if there is any "real" competition for the deal. You might be able to discount the "unnamed parties" allegedly lurking in the shadows. Lack of real competition tends to lower the price and sweeten other terms for the buyer. When the deal is chasing you the points of negotiating leverage for the buyer should be clearer.

I hate to say this again, but deal-making is a little like dating while seriously looking for a life partner. It is hard to evaluate the qualifications and suitability of candidates unless you've seen a fair number of them. The more experience in the process the more selective the choices become to test the seriousness of the relationship - with the hope that they might become permanent. But, if you are chasing a date, or if the date is chasing you, there is a pretty good chance that all the wrong signals will be sent and the relationship won't mature. Don't press too hard. Let the deals, like the good partners in life, come to you so that you can understand and appreciate them thoughtfully.

10

THE DEALS YOU DON'T DO, DON'T HURT YOU

There is a certain momentum to deal-making that becomes infectious. In fact, I've observed extreme behavior by individuals who could be characterized as "deal junkies." It must be the thrill of the hunt. Or, perhaps it is the idea that someone can "win" a deal – whether that means outgunning a competitor or actually squeezing the deal so hard that it becomes one-sided. Within the deal culture, there are many enablers who are quite content to keep feeding the habit of the deal junkie – brokers, consultants, investment bankers, etc. In fact, it is their job and life's mission to do just that, because they get a piece of the action.

So, a note of caution is worth at least one chapter in this book. Because, you don't have to complete a deal, unless you really want to. And, generally speaking, the deals you don't do, don't hurt you. In fact, the deals you don't do probably never hurt you (or your business). It is worth referring back to Chapter 8, to be reminded that "you never run out of deals."

Why is this warning necessary for everyone, not just executives, to embrace? There is one simple reason. Because *the deals you do can actually hurt you.*

If an executive were to fall in love with the deal-making process, or the false sense of accomplishment in getting a deal done, he may forget that fundamental principle. Deals are done to make money. If your judgment is impaired in any fashion, making money as the outcome becomes increasingly difficult. It is hard enough to do good deals when you have all your faculties. The process demands intensive focus and attention to detail when a deal is being evaluated and then committed to an agreement. You wouldn't encourage either your negotiating team or your lawyers to try to do this while drunk, would you? So, why act a though you are drunk on another type of elixir?

The other reality is that many deals that initially look good turn sour in the later stages of negotiations. It would be good to walk away when that happens (assuming that you legally are able to do this). Again, the deals you don't do don't hurt you – but the ones you do can hurt you.

And, don't just invoke this advice if you are working only on large transactions. Sometimes it is valid to apply the adage to the mundane transactions that populate your day to day decisions. For example, one common occurrence is hiring a new employee. On one level this is just another deal to be made. Sometimes in the process of trying to hire a person a manager settles for an incompetent person, perhaps because they are trying to avoid the continued pain of having an open position and a stressed staff. But, why make a bad hire? Again, you never run out of people to hire (although the process of finding the right person may take some time). But if a person doesn't meet the thresholds of: 1) competency,

2) attitude and 3) fit – you are probably making a bad deal. This will ultimately cost you money. And, you'll be back where you started anyway, in another cycle of deal making.

So, repeat after me: "The deals I don't do, don't hurt me."

11

NEGOTIATION SHOULD BE
AN "AWAY GAME"

I know the advice in the title is counter-intuitive. But that is why it may also be a good approach.

The working theory is that when you are negotiating as the buyer, you should put the onus for all the details onto the seller including the location for all meetings and the closing. This is the equivalent of making this an "away game" for you, versus a "home game." We get conditioned by sports to believe that the home team has the advantage (in the NBA, the home teams win over 60% of the games over the course of a full season). But, the thinking doesn't necessarily translate well to deal-making.

Sellers like the comfort of thinking that they are in charge. It is often an illusion that the buyer is well-served by, and may be able to convert into full delusion. The process of selling is very often the result of an operational shortcoming or a fundamental change in the value of an enterprise or asset. Surprisingly few assets get sold at, or near, the peak of their value. But many do get sold when fortunes are declining, or when cleaning up "the books" is the goal. The sellers, generally invested with past behavior, may have some remorse. In fact, they probably will. Letting them believe that they are actually in control of the process, reduces seller's remorse and makes things go more smoothly. It reduces stress (or guilt).

Pragmatically, buyers can often win more substantial deal points if it appears they are making concessions on other deal points – the classic "give and take." The flow of documents and the venue for closing a deal can be major deal points from the seller's viewpoint. If so, the buyer can get "something" for giving up nothing of practical value.

Now, here's a more important legal point, provided with a disclaimer. I'm not attempting to provide legal services or advice. Probably the buyer shouldn't write the legal documents involved, or write any part of them which are incorporated into definitive agreements. Legally, the common interpretation (especially if it is unclear) of an agreement resides as a right to the party that is not the "maker" of a contract. This point is very important. I was personally involved in a legal proceeding with many millions of dollars in dispute. I represented the buyer in negotiating the original business deal but had no hand in the final written documents, terms of which became subject to differing interpretations many years later. At a critical point in the trial the judge looked at me directly (I was under oath) and asked: "Were your fingers ever on the keyboard when any part of this document was written?" Fortunately, I could honestly answer no. If I had provided an answer with less clarity the fate of the entire case would have been altered. Our side prevailed.

Following the above advice is a little tricky. You definitely will need lawyers involved on your side to get all the "boilerplate" in order. Your lawyers will talk to their lawyers in the process of doing this. But, as pertains to the essence of the actual "deal points," it has been my experience to keep those communications at the deal-maker level. They get resolved faster. Most of it is verbal. Beware of e-mail. There is better protection if you aren't writing the actual terms, using your keyboard.

Resist the natural inclination to control a deal if you are the buyer. Remember, you are already in control because you have the power to walk away. Moreover, your chances for favorable horse-trading improve dramatically if you have structured this as a "home game" for the seller and an "away game" for you. You goal is to obtain maximum value. Civility can be a strong tool in your toolbox.

12

YOU MUST FLINCH
TO MAKE A GOOD DEAL

The most important measure of a good deal is whether you (as either buyer or seller) have received expected value, or at least fair value, after the transaction has closed. You may not know this for sure at the time you make the exchange, generally of "money" for "something." Even being convinced that you "won" a deal doesn't mean much. Both parties might have the same point of view. Ego isn't an accurate barometer.

So, how can you have some comfort, or any comfort, that you made the best deal possible? There is one technique that helps. *You must flinch.* I don't mean a little flinch. I mean that you draw the figurative "line in the sand" and you are prepared to walk away. The purpose of the flinch is to test the resolve of the other party and to stop the negotiating process pre-maturely. Some believe that the longer the process of negotiating goes on, the higher the probability that the buyer loses ground. Others would contend that the seller loses. What is true is that the weaker party tends to be strong-armed by the stronger party over time. A flinch communicates that you aren't a weak negotiator.

How hard is this to do? It depends. If you absolutely need the deal, then walking away might be disastrous. But, teletyping your "must have" position to the other side can be just as disastrous. So even in this situation a good, hard flinch will be useful. The attractive thing about flinching is that you have the option to reverse your position, if necessary.

But if you don't absolutely need the deal to close and especially if you believe (as I do) that there are always other deals to be done, why not give my suggestion a try? You literally have nothing to lose and lots to gain. This is especially true for commodity-type items – like homes, cars, hard assets and even employees to some extent. Set your limit price and terms. Then see what happens.

Now a word about technique. To flinch, many people believe that they must be mean-spirited. Or sometimes, the demeanor of being mean is considered part of the persona that must be adopted to actually introduce the flinch. Being mean really doesn't help a buyer and it never helps the seller. In fact, with experienced negotiators meanness can send a deal "over the cliff" into oblivion. Remember, there are negotiators (like me) who believe you can't do a good deal with a bad person. The technique that I have seen masterfully performed is the flinch, encased in civility, delivered with a calm voice. For example: "You really have an attractive property for sale, but I must absolutely live within this maximum price for it to make sense to us. I'm very hopeful that we can reach some agreement. If not, I'll need to move on and wait for another opportunity. I must do this in fairness to my investors."

Now for advanced technique. The flinch works even better when you casually, but again civilly, infer that you are also evaluating other deals and you have only enough funds to make one deal. This works even better when this is true! Creating the sense that "the fish might spit the hook" is a very effective flinch hardener. And, you don't have to be mean to do it. But you have to be committed to making a good deal.

Now for one last point. You only get one flinch. If you win the deal point because of the flinch, don't (I repeat, don't) try to go back and try flinching for a progression of other deal points. Remember, the flinch is meant to shut down the negotiation process. Going back with other "must haves" will be read (correctly) as negotiating in bad-faith.

None-the-less, some deal makers thrive on the reputation that they've earned as "grinders" – which means they constantly flinch. Once that word gets around, they are deluding themselves into thinking that they have achieved maximum value. The market simply adjusts to their behavior. The negotiations begin and end differently.

Nice people have a better chance of consistently making better deals – especially if they combine being nice with good research and intelligent analysis. But it is essential that even nice people flinch one time, and mean it.

SECTION III
PRACTICE WISE

13

THE 80-20 RULE APPLIES ABOUT 80% OF THE TIME

People refer to the 80-20 Rule quite often, both in business and in everyday conversation. What is generally meant is that the first, or most important, 80% of knowledge or impact can by achieved with the first 20% of the effort or resources expended.

There are common variations on a theme. One is that 80% of the work on a project is done by 20% of the people involved. Charitable projects universally prove this rule. Another is that the first 80% of all buyers of a good or service will be from a hard core 20% of the overall customer population. Statistical data are often presented in 80-20 terms. For example, the top 20% income families pay 80% of the income taxes (a close approximation to reality in the U.S.). You can probably think of other instances where the 80-20 Rule has been applied to data in your work or life experiences.

The 80-20 Rule is useful because it can be accurate in describing macro behavior. In fact, it may be surprisingly accurate in 80% of such cases. That means it isn't very accurate at all in the other 20% (yet another ironic twist on the 80-20 Rule).

The question worth asking is: Why is the 80-20 Rule part of our culture? More importantly, why does it seem to apply to so many situations? Statisticians could have a field day with this question and they may be able effortlessly to debunk the entire concept. But I suspect that even they would come to some conclusions that would support the validity of the 80-20 Rule, at least in situations involving human behavior.

Here's my theory. The general population and the skill sets they embody actually fall neatly into quintiles (100% divided into five equal quintiles of 20% each). There is an exceptional 20% of any large enough sample that performs in an exceptionally distinctive manner. This leaves an 80% remainder that doesn't act exceptionally. This becomes a natural 80-20 Rule. Conversely, at the bottom quintile there are 20% who perform in an exceptionally negative fashion. Thus another natural 80-20 Rule emerges. The folks in the middle ranges of the population really aren't defining incremental trends and tend to align into the category of the least remarkable quintiles on either side – positive or negative as the case may be. At least this is one layman's attempt to explain the 80-20 Rule.

What does the 80-20 Rule mean for the manager or the executive? First and foremost, it means that you can get a lot done with modest resources – at least the first time around. Skunkworks prove the rule. To use a golf analogy, you can usually get the ball on the green (close enough to see the cup) with a couple of strokes. Getting the ball into the cup (perfection) then becomes challenging, as putting in golf tends to be. So, push to get the first blast of results out of your organization with a sense of urgency. It is always surprising just how much can be accomplished in a short amount of time. The stars on any team will naturally accomplish sizable blocks of work if they aren't handicapped by the negative influence of the worst performers. The folks in the middle will go along for the ride – at least in short intervals.

An interesting sequence to follow for maximum results is to apply the 80-20 Rule to the same work or project in consecutive bursts (versus an endless continuum). After getting the project "ball on the green," the second effort burst might well get you 80% of the distance from the end of the first project to the eventual goal. Mathematically, that would be 80%, plus another 16% (80% of the remaining 20%), or 96% to the goal line. That's pretty darned good for most business endeavors.

The 80-20 Rule also illuminates an embedded warning worth heading. Perfection is very rarely achieved. Actually striving for perfection isn't that useful. For example, every business decision would be perfect if all the data were perfect. And, every business would be performing at maximum capacity if all the employees were the very best available at their positions. Realistically, that never happens. The great executives achieve results with available resources, but with uncommon attention to focus and results. Great executives aren't surprised by the lack of organizational perfection and they never use it as an excuse. But, they tend to be very hard on themselves and their immediate reporting line – their top 20% performers.

14

PUT A CATFISH IN THE HOLD

I don't remember where I read this fictional story, but the lesson is one I've never forgotten. Here's how it goes:

There was a commercial fisherman working the New England Coast who had a reputation for always bringing in the freshest catch. The other fishermen from the same port were jealous of this fact because this man's fish were always purchased first and at premium prices. They had to admit that this wasn't just an unsubstantiated perception – that his fish were fresher – but an accepted fact. And, the other fishermen just couldn't figure out how this one person was able to consistently deliver a superior product to the marketplace. They all fished in the same waters. Their equipment was essentially the same. They used the same nets. In fact, on every visible measure, everyone should have delivered exactly the same quality of fish to market – especially when averaged over long measurement periods. Yet, everyone agreed that this one fisherman had a secret for success that nobody understood or could replicate.

After many successful years, the fisherman was queried on his deathbed. The other fishermen wanted to know his "secret" before he passed into the next life. One brave soul finally asked the burning question: "How were you able to consistently deliver fresher fish to market, when all of us were using the same boats and equipment and we all saw your boat in exactly the same waters that we fished in?"

The dying man finally revealed his secret. He said that before he left port he always put a fresh catfish into his empty hold. The catfish was an aggressive fish that tended to nip at all the other fish dumped into the hold and even ate a few during an extended voyage. But the presence of the catfish in the hold made the other fish more alert and more active – in their attempt not to be victimized by the predator. So, he lost a few fish along the way. By the time he got into port the remaining fish were just fresher.

There are many opportunities in business to figurative-ly "put a catfish in the hold." Consistent with the fisherman's story, sometimes this "catfish" will nip at a few of the "status quo fish" and perhaps identify a couple that shouldn't survive the voyage. But, overall the catfish will make everyone more alert and active with the result that something above the expected norm should result.

Almost always, *the catfish needs to be an outsider.* Sometimes new blood in an organization is what is needed to get "off the dime." The new person can act as a catalyst. Isn't the "catfish" story really a metaphor for what often happens in business when results are sub-par and things need to be shaken up? The new hires are brought in to change things around with the hope of making improvements.

Of course, the alternate type of catfish is the hired gun – the outsider with no internal constituency, but with the specific mission to shake things up. These people are called consultants. Some are very good and serve their client businesses well. Some have acquired the deserved reputation of being expensive, long-winded, and impractical (meaning that their advice really can't be implemented). The best ones work with the captain of the figurative fishing boat to bring in a fresh catch. They make something happen fast, with as few casualties as possible. As a result, they aren't beloved by the retained workforce because they push too hard and don't have to live with the long-term effects of hurt feelings.

At the risk of taking the metaphor beyond its useful lesson, executives need to consistently have a catfish in the hold. They also must change-out the catfish with regularity to obtain maximum value. Eventually, a single catfish might start to mimic the behavior of the more passive fish. The weight of organizations naturally reverts to the mean in matters of comfort, protectionism and lower performance standards.

But, the story makes a strong case for the value of fresher fish to the marketplace and for fishermen attempting to deliver what the marketplace is buying – including the use of outsiders, if that's what it takes.

15

AT LEAST 50% OF THE
PEOPLE ARE BELOW AVERAGE

This was one of my father's favorite sayings. It made a big impression on me when I was sixteen and learning to drive. He reminded me that at least 50% of the drivers on the road with me were below average. The message: be careful, son and drive defensively. Of course, he never went so far as to remind me that as soon as I got my license I would automatically be one of the people in the lower 50%. I only felt that particular terror when I was the father of a sixteen year-old driver.

There is an ironic elegance to the saying that *at least* 50% of the people in any situation are below average. There is also an embedded challenge for each person to determine if they are in the category of being below average. This concept is especially difficult for intelligent and successful people to absorb because in their minds nothing they do is below average. We'll dispel that myth in a moment.

First, let's talk about the statistical reality. Of course, exactly 50% of the people are below average in any situation, assuming a large enough sample. This fact is important to remember in every aspect of business – from consumer behavior, to marketing, to sales. It is most obviously on display regarding internal company communication. Messages that are obvious to decision makers (often inherently smart) aren't always so obvious to the people receiving them. Think of the audience located near a radio tower. Not everyone is exactly on the same frequency as the nearest station. In fact, most people aren't even dialed-in to a single station. Even when they are, there is plentiful interference and static to confuse things.

Managers get frustrated when something they say or do isn't understood. The inclination is to cast blame on the "dummies" that "just don't get it." But who is really at fault if a smart person knows that at least 50% of the audience being communicated with is below average? With repeated lack of success, a smart manager may actually come to the revelation that they are in the lower 50% as communicators. Behavioral change is required to advance into the upper 50%.

Now comes my favorite part of the saying – the "at least" modifier. I think my father had it right, in any situation at least 50% are below average. That means that in every situation, no more than 50% are above average. But that number could be quite a bit smaller. Here's the thinking. At any moment in time, even the most intelligent or talented person is probably not "on their game." They may be distracted in some way. So, even the best among us can fall into the lower 50% with ease through lack of attention. Smart people have automobile accidents for dumb reasons. For example, smart people use cell phones while driving, which are statistically proven to increase the probability of an accident. Why do they do this? I don't know. But, I think it is proof that my dad had it right.

The rule is a bit humbling because it applies to every single situation in life. It is hard to be above average at everything. The smartest guy in the world can't will himself to be great at golf. In fact, some of the best athletes in the world can't will themselves to be great at golf. With this example, it is easy to prove, although difficult to acknowledge, that each of us is below average in many situations – often well below average. This self-realization is important for making a commitment to improve. But it also provides guidance for us to function in daily life. Would you decide on your own medical treatment (maybe) and then perform surgery on yourself (never)? No, we go to doctors (who are generally way above average in intelligence but aren't particularly good at golf). Similarly, do doctors think that they can solve mechanical issues on their own vehicles? I know a number of doctors who are in awe of their car mechanics.

One of the most obvious examples of this rule applies to stock picking. Among the category of experts that manage mutual funds, about 70% fail to achieve the automatic returns of index funds in a given year. These are well-trained, experienced and self-proclaimed experts. And, over two-thirds of them are consistently below average.

It might be wise to consider this adage when you are immersed into a new situation with a group of strangers. There's a good chance that you are in the lower 50%. But, it may not serve you well if everyone knew that. This would be a good time to keep your head down, buy some time and then figure out how to raise your standing.

16

No whining allowed

Somewhere I saw this phrase made into sign. I wish I could remember where it was. The message is direct and clear. I'd like to make up signs like this myself to pass out. I'd need a large supply.

We all dislike being in the presence of a whiner: someone making those all-too-common shrill and unpleasant comments that really don't need to be communicated. We avoid the person with a personality that is defined by their tendency to whine about everything. The whiner is the complainer with "an attitude." Usually they have nothing of substance to complain about.

So, why would we ever reward whining in business? We shouldn't. But we tend to overlook it more in a work situation that we would in interactions with our friends. For starters, you can't escape the work situations. Whereas, you may always select your friends. Whiners make terrible friends.

Whining is selfish behavior. It is only slightly better than passive-aggressive behavior. This is only because there is actually some verbal message being communicated about what is wrong or upsetting. Generally the complaint is insignificant. And the listener quickly discounts all that is being said by type-casting the whiner. The targets are predictable. One common theme is to vent on the troubles that seem to be caused by a manager or a fellow employee. Whining is a big excuse. The people that whine are so used to doing it that they don't realize that it diminishes them and their message to the point of being inconsequential. They think they are being honest. But honest people don't whine. They attack things head on and find workable solutions.

Whining is an organizational virus. Once a single person does it and it isn't checked, then a larger group tends to mimic the behavior. And so on, and so on. Then whining has the power to be destructive, negating the positive messages and behaviors that are the hallmarks of really healthy organizations.

Whining must be checked immediately. Your enterprise can't afford to accept it as part of the culture. You know that there is really a problem when you start whining about all the whining being done. Ouch!

I really wish I could remember where I first saw this sign. Simply genius.

17

THE BEST WAY TO
GET EVEN IS TO FORGET

Holding grudges is a time-honored tradition across all generations and cultures. In my experience, it is also a complete waste of time in today's business environment. Let it go.

The problems that create hard feelings are wrapped in three different packages. First, there is so much volume in business activity and high-velocity change which it is inevitable that personal sensitivities may become irritated. Second, when money is involved there are cross-currents of individual personality, greed and fear. All of these play into the uncertainties that create misplaced expectations and personal stress. Third, there are actually bad people out there, and their activities are totally self-serving and exclude the sensitivities and the sense of justice that most folks naturally embrace. There is no shortage of bad people, so it makes sense to avoid doing business with them if you can.

But try as you might to avoid getting buffeted around in business, it is inevitable that this will happen. It happens to chief executives, senior executives, line management, and employees alike. Nobody is exempt. When it happens, you'll probably be angry.

How to handle disappointments, ill-will and tragedies are challenges that everyone in business must address at some point. Sometimes you might actually get some measure of justice through the legal system. But, that is a source of satisfaction that I've come to believe is capricious at best, and always time-consuming and expensive. Relying on courts is unworthy of high expectations or very much emotional investment.

The first question to ask yourself is if the injustice you are harboring is real or concocted. Sometimes we blame our personal failures on others. There must be a culprit if I am the victim. Just as often, the perceived injustice is the result of a personal lack of preparation, understanding or inattention. The person we should be angry with is ourselves. When this is the case, converting the energy into behavioral change has the real potential to be valuable for a lifetime.

But, sometimes negative events do happen to us. Sometimes they are inflicted by others. What is the point of trying to find the culprit and then trying to inflict an equal amount of pain back their way? Not much. It is a drain of productive time and the positive forces of creativity that should be harnessed for your future success. This is the ultimate test of "cutting your losses."

The game is over. Regroup and get prepared to play another game (figuratively) the next day. As my high school buddy, Col. Jack Klevecz (U.S. Army, Retired), used to say: "You win some. You lose some. Some get rained out. But, you suit-up for'em all."

18

THE TWO MOST POWERFUL WORDS ARE: "THANK YOU"

I wish this chapter were unnecessary. But it isn't. It is painful to point to the culprit – a lack of manners and civility. But, it is evident that we must. Are parents just not teaching the fundamental courtesies of living in society? Are schools not reinforcing the tenets of acceptable social behavior? Are people of all ages just so self-absorbed that they forget some of the niceties that lubricate personal interactions? Or worse yet, maybe they don't care. Who knows what the cause is. I don't.

But, I do know one thing for certain. If you want to distinguish yourself above the crowd, you only have to do one simple thing – just say "thank you" when appropriate. And mean it.

In business it is a rare event to hear the words "thank you" and rarer still to see them in writing. Perhaps it is the fault of how business is portrayed in the media, especially in the movies or on TV. The successful business man is written into these scripts as a mean-spirited individual who would run over his mother for a dollar. I call this the "J.R. Ewing School of Management Syndrome" (remember J.R. from the *Dallas* television series?). But, the later day versions of popular TV shows are no better. Donald Trump is known for saying: "You're fired" – with a grimace and with an attitude. Has anyone ever heard him say "thank you" on TV? It is too bad for Trump, and too bad for all of us that have to live with the insensitive perceptions reinforced in a society that has come to distrust and despise business. As a result, an emerging generation of managers and business leaders is adopting this warped ethic and actually fulfilling the vision by becoming brash, uncaring, self-absorbed business practitioners.

Absolutely the biggest impression is created when you say "thank you" in writing (by hand is great) and mailed in a note to the recipient. Receiving mail by post is considered more impactful in a world of ubiquitous e-mail messaging. If you only do one thing after reading this book, go out and purchase some personalized note cards and get into the habit of sending out one sincere note per week to the people that make your life better. The returns on this investment will be enormous. I promise you. Small, but thoughtful gifts with the note will put you in the "Business Civility Hall of Fame." Nobody forgets it.

As we'll mention elsewhere, in "marketing" it is great to have one of the three major share-of-mind positions: first, best or different. The great thing about saying "thank you" is that you can own all three positions. The impression that this simple act creates is much larger than it should be.

But, don't bother to give any thanks to Hollywood, J.R. Ewing, or Donald Trump.

19

BEING A BALLPLAYER AIN'T HARD, IF YOU'RE A BALLPLAYER

I have vivid memories of visiting the Baseball Hall of Fame in Cooperstown on a very cold and snowy weekday in late December, many years ago. I was driving from Massachusetts to Cincinnati with my family and we decided to stop on the way for an overnight in Upstate New York. When the doors to the museum opened we were the very first to enter. Only a handful of visitors arrived that entire morning, due to the severe weather which continued to rage outside.

In those days (we haven't been back recently) there was a small theatre that everyone was expected to enter before they were able to roam the premises. There, they presented a very well-produced film which provided background and texture to the game of baseball. Even my wife liked the show, which is saying something. Of course, my son and I were in heaven. In one part of the presentation they featured historical photographs of early ballplayers with voiced-over quotations. The presentation may even have been a shortened version of the well-known Ken Burns' documentary on the game. So, there was this sepia picture of a ballplayer in one of those ancient baggy uniforms and a resonant voice that claimed: "Being a ballplayer ain't hard . . . if you're a ballplayer." It is something I've never forgotten.

I'm reminded of that phrase constantly when I'm working with managers and executives. This is because, with simple word substitution, a profound truth emerges: "Being a manager ain't hard, if you're a manager."

So, now a debate begins. Can management skills be taught and learned? Or, is management something that only comes naturally? Are you born with management genes, or can you manufacture them? This is "nature versus nurture" in a business context.

If you are expecting the answer, you are expecting a little too much from your modest investment in this book. I'm not a researcher, or a social scientist, or a medical practitioner. Even if I were, I'm not sure there is a definitive answer to the question.

But, I am an alert observer of people. I see lots of managers in working situations. I can tell you without a doubt that some men and women are just plain better at managing than others are. And, it has nothing to do with being smart. I've seen some great managers that are far from having great intellects. I've also seen some terrible managers with outstanding grades from top schools or with top performance reviews in individual contributor roles.

Here's where my observations lead me. Every good manager I've ever known has really wanted to manage people and events. Actually, that isn't quite right. Lots of people in business want to be managers, just like every kid wants to be the pitcher at Little League tryouts. *The really great managers cherish the job because they thrive on the constant challenges of the job.* Because they have an obsession for the job they have either acquired the skills to overcome their weaknesses, or they have enhanced their natural abilities through hard work. They have a genuine concern for people and they keep trying to get the most productivity out of a team. They understand the power of focus and that finite resources need to be deployed with efficiency. They know that there is always somebody watching their performance and they over-achieve as a way to get "applause" from their audience. Being a good manager ain't hard. It's not because the process of being good isn't hard, it's because the process is something they have a passion for. So, in the mind of a talented manager, it ain't hard.

Regrettably, not everyone is cut out to become a manager. There is no shame in that realization. In fact, that realization may help many of you toward a better quality of life through satisfaction as individual contributors. That might relieve the stress of doing something you really don't like. Can you be a doctor if you really can't tolerate the sight of blood? Can you be an accountant if you really don't like adding and subtracting numbers? The answers are obvious. But there is an unfortunate expectation that at some point everyone deserves a crack at being "the boss." It isn't uncommon for someone to achieve this status and eventually realize it is one of the unluckiest days of their life.

The great news about working for businesses or organizations is that not everyone has to be a manager. There are countless roles and positions to play that add value. So, everyone can actually be a ballplayer in a figurative sense – in other words, play their position well. With this perspective you will find a place to work at something you love. Therefore, you'll be inclined to be good at it.

So, aren't we are back where we started on a snowy day in Cooperstown? "Being a ballplayer ain't hard, if you're a ballplayer."

SECTION IV
FOCUS WISE

20

THE TOUGHEST PERSON TO MANAGE IS YOURSELF

Never mind managing Babe Ruth (see Chapter 60). Managing him would be easy compared to managing yourself. At least that is my experience.

As presented elsewhere (see Chapter 56), there is only one kind of motivation – self-motivation. So, the trick is how to motivate yourself to do the things you inherently don't want to do, even when you know they need to be done. You are, in a very real sense, in conflict with yourself.

Sometimes it is nature over intellect (I really don't want to mow the lawn – I'd rather rest and watch S*ports Center*). Sometimes it requires mind over matter (I really don't want to do my income taxes, but it is required). The demons abound, all telling you to act in one way, while the muses are telling the opposite story. But the conflicts remain. How does one internally referee a winner and a loser? One of the simple answers (or excuses) for poor behavior or poor performance is that with any decision at least one of your inner desires is satisfied. So who is stronger, the muse or the demon?

The goal in business is to do the things as a leader or an executive that will serve the organization and also serve your primal needs. It gets complicated. Just ask the folks involved with Enron. Sure, it may not happen on the scale of Enron or some of the other classic business failures fueled by personal greed. But, it isn't all that hard to talk yourself into doing the wrong thing. Executives and managers are consistently doing the wrong things on little matters, with convenient self-justification. They have a very tough time managing themselves. Managing others is easy, often instinctive. Managing yourself is hard and quite often counter-instinctive.

The only way out for most leaders is to have a good road map. Again, this sounds simple, but it isn't. This is because most people can't be trusted to draw their own roadmap. They need someone else to do it for them. It is true that everyone ultimately has a boss; so many executives look to the boss (sometimes the governing body, like a Board of Directors) for guidance. Some hire consultants to put a plan together that the organization will salute and that they can follow with confidence. Some look to self-help books for direction and answers. Authors and bookstores like this option (and I'm beginning to see the light). Some turn to philosophy or to religion and try to frame their actions against a proven code of behavior. These are all valid methods to overcome the bias toward self-delusion. But, too many people just never get it right.

As a consultant, I frequently use the tool of telling stories. I've actually gotten quite good at making up parables. I often use characters and circumstances that are created to draw my clients into the problems of other people, when in fact I'm describing their situations with a disguise. It is amazing how a smart, well-trained executive will gravitate immediately to solving someone else's problem – usually in the most direct, ethical and efficient manner. They take pleasure in demonstrating to me how smart, or how tough, or how principled they are in the face of adversity. They love doing my job for me and proving that they are smartest person in the room.

Then comes the "gotcha." They actually have done my job. They have solved their own problem. Their own advice is valid and brilliant. My job should be done. There is a plan. It is a plan generated by the executive for his or her own behavior. It is usually a good, or at least a workable, plan. There are benchmarks to measure success against. Everything is the way it should be according to all the textbooks. Chalk up another consulting success.

This is where it becomes evident that managing yourself is the hardest task of all. The demons start to knock on the door. The plan is diluted. The benchmarks aren't met and the excuses become creative. Getting back on track takes some intervention by a superior or a trusted confidant. Self-medication is nearly impossible because self-motivation is conflicted.

Admit it. Managing yourself is the hardest of all management tasks. Get some help and welcome it. If you manage to do that one thing you might have a chance.

21

THERE ARE FOUR PHASES OF EVOLUTION INTO A NEW JOB

Part of the backdrop for modern business is the constant change of responsibilities, assignments and jobs. Transitions are important components of business practice that need to be managed and optimized. Good executives are always in a constant state of redefining themselves, either internally at their existing companies, or externally as they accept new jobs in new companies and sometimes in new industries. Yet as important as transitions are, there is substantial ignorance, even among smart people, as to what to expect from a new employee. Or closer to home, what you should expect if you are the new employee?

There are four easy-to-distinguish phases of transition. I didn't invent these. But, I've observed them many times and I'm surprised how universal and predictable they are. Once I share these phases with you, you'll readily see the same patterns that you have witnessed or experienced yourself. If you are currently in a transition the patterns will strike very close to home.

Phase 1
You don't know what you don't know.

Immediately after you take a new assignment or position, you are dumped into the deep end of the Phase 1 swimming pool. My longtime friend and Wharton classmate, Harry Kangis, calls this being "unconsciously incompetent." I've heard others refer to it in similar ways. Often you are so uninformed or naïve that you actually don't know that you don't know what you don't know (read this again slowly until you get it). People think they are hired or promoted because they are smart and can be effective on the very first day. That is rarely possible. Making decisions while you are in this phase of evolution is risky and dangerous. You are almost guaranteed to make a mistake, because you (literally) don't know what you don't know. The proper course of action is to move as quickly as possible to Phase 2. The way to get there is simple enough. Make friends with all of the people in the organization you'll depend upon for success (up, down and sideways) and listen to what they tell you when you ask them for advice on how to succeed at your new job. When you are hiring a new person, structure the first few weeks so that the new person is forced to do this. Failing to do this almost always means ultimately failing at the new job. "Do-overs" are messy.

Phase 2
You do know what you don't know.

This is the scariest phase because you are overwhelmed by the necessary learning curve ahead. But one good sign is that you are getting through Phase 1. My friend Harry would refer to this phase as being "consciously incompetent." The course of action, here again, is to accelerate the process to the next phase. This takes the fearless appetite to identify all the areas that you need to fill with knowledge, people or other resources. So, make a list of the things you don't know, because this knowledge is power.

A few trusted confidants can help you get through this phase faster. Consultants can be helpful. What you are looking for is the kind of honesty that a spouse will provide – pretty straightforward. Then start back-filling frantically against the voids.

Phase 3
You do know what you should know.

You'll emerge from Phase 2 and pass through Phase 3 incrementally. Little by little, the voids in knowledge and experience will be filled. In the cases where there can be "patches" (adding outside resources to fill the holes) you'll start creating them. As you pass through Phase 3, you'll begin exhaling for the first time, and deep sleep will come easier. Some might say that you are never really through Phase 3, because there is a constant barrage of new challenges that must be faced in the dynamic workplace. Fair enough. When you are making progress in this phase you are becoming "consciously competent." Don't pat yourself on the back too hard, because the ultimate goal is Phase 4, and you may not be there yet.

Phase 4
You don't think about what you do or don't know.

This is the "sweet spot" for success, which isn't achieved across the board – but starts to include the important areas of responsibility requiring decisions. You hit this last phase when you are able to do effective things at your new position by "instinct." Great executives and leaders are very instinctive about their jobs. When they are right, these instincts also breed confidence which is transferred down into the team.

Here is a warning. If you start a new position using old instincts for a new assignment you are in serious danger of making a mess of things. It may be obvious to all concerned that you are actually in Phase 1, while you may not be smart enough to know it. There are no short-cuts. You will go through all four phases every time you take on a new role. The game is to get through them all as fast as possible.

22

THERE ARE TWO PARTS
TO EVERY DECISION

There are two parts to every business decision of consequence. They are: 1) what is the right thing to do? And, 2) how do you do Part 1, well?

This breakdown of decision making into component parts isn't something new, and it is not my invention. I've seen some variation of this theme many times in business literature, so much so that I couldn't begin to provide attribution. I will tell you that this is a piece of guidance that I promote liberally in my consulting work. It just makes so much sense. As with so many pieces of good advice, it is rare when you meet someone who consistently puts the advice into practice.

The very first pothole on the road to embracing this guidance is the tendency for most people to delay decisions under the delusion that by delaying they will actually increase their probability of making the correct decision. Executives and managers aren't immune from the disease. Once in a while this tactic actually works. So the propensity to procrastinate gains practical favor and acceptance. I'm not even suggesting that this is wrong.

What I will suggest (again, it's in all the literature) is *that avoiding a decision is in fact the same as making a decision not to act at a given moment in time.*

Fortunately in business, unlike trauma surgery, most of the decisions don't have to be instantaneous. Gathering more and better data can be a legitimate reason for postponing a decision. But the act of delaying is in itself a decision and perhaps it is an important one. Beyond a certain point the data rarely get that much more accurate and the chances of making a good decision actually stumble into the zone of diminishing returns. Time is of the essence to some degree.

So, step one is bringing yourself to the point of making a decision and then using your best judgment to definitively make it. There is so much that can be written about the decision-making process that it would be unfair, and potentially harmful, to provide specific guidance in a short chapter. But what can be said with a fair amount of instinctive accuracy is that the process of decision making is muddled because of the procedural circumstances (all the so-called "hair") that accompany making the decision.

What do I mean? Take a classic example. The figurative "Joe" needs to be terminated because his performance is poor, and his attitude is even worse. So, a decision about Joe's future is timely. But the decision makers have other things to consider. 1) How will his fellow employees react? 2) How will Joe's work get done? 3) Is Joe likely to sue the company? Or, 4) How will Joe take care of his family if he is fired? The questions are almost limitless if you are trying to avoid the actual confrontation when Joe is given the pink slip, or you are trying to avoid the internal disruption of finding a replacement.

So somebody conveniently comes along and says: "Why don't we give Joe another sixty days and see how he does, and then make the decision?" This is just one example of the kind of non-decision decision that is made all the time – precisely because the "yes or no" is confused with the "how to" of the decision making process. In my experience, Joe rarely improves (we address this in Chapter 65, *Change the Person in Thirty Days*).

Now think about the same situation as actually having two parts. The first part of the decision is whether or not Joe should keep his job. If the evidence is compelling that he should be terminated, then the decision should be made to do exactly that. Only then does the second part of the decision process begin – how Joe will be terminated. This is where the considerations that are in the best interest of the company or organization are labeled, sorted and executed. The required output of this process is a plan that can be followed to implement the initial decision.

By dividing the decision-making process into two parts, it is actually easier to get both parts of the decision right – enhancing the overall proficiency of the decision making process.

So, what happens if the decision is made, it is executed according to plan, and it turns out to be wrong? It only means that it is time for another, or other, decisions to be made. Very rare is the case where a decision can be undone without any consequences. So this isn't a logical path to follow initially. It is better to view the entire process with a fresh approach and to follow the same two-step process all over again.

Life is a progression of decisions that need to be made. The important ones need to be divided into two parts.

23

ORGANIZATIONS ARE LIKE TREES — THEY DIE FROM THE TOP DOWN

This is a time-proven observation which business leaders are reluctant to acknowledge. When organizations are in distress the fault is almost always at the top – the small group of senior executives that control or run things. This is especially true if they have been there for a while and the decline has happened steadily on their watch. This would seem so obvious that it wouldn't be necessary for a dedicated chapter in this book. The reason that a chapter is needed is the "blame game."

When things don't go well there is a tendency by the top guys to push the blame into the deepest crevices of the organization, working from the bottom up. If executives are watching the gauges on their dashboard (as they should be), the senior guys are the very first to know that results are disappointing and which way they are headed (up or down) in the near future. They will either fix the situation or they won't. Business is a world of bifurcated events. If they fix it – they are doing their jobs and deserve the credit. If they don't fix it, the consequences are their fault – plain and simple.

The reason why things die from the top down is because the guys at the top are the only ones with both the power and the incentives to change things. Again, this is such a simple concept to understand, but it is often hidden in the smokescreen of the moment. And, it becomes complicated by the personalities involved (see *Borbely's Rule* about politics, Chapter 54).

So, how is the game is played in the real world? Once failure is identified, the first inclination is to blame somebody else. Usually the first to be blamed are persons very deep in the organization. Some of these people are dead wood and some have bad attitude. These are people that probably should have been terminated long ago. It takes the fear of failure to actually make it happen. This part of the process is usually good for an organization and oftentimes buys enough time, or helps the bottom line enough, to create the illusion of invigorated senior management. You can read about this practically every day in the business press. "Company (fill in the name here) to cut back workforce to become more competitive in the marketplace." Nobody ever seems to ask a very important question. What was this senior management team doing one year, one month or even one week before this watershed announcement?

When the "force reduction" medicine doesn't do the job, the next level of blame gets dropped onto middle management. This takes a bit longer because of the transitive law – there are direct linkages between senior and junior managers creating awkward accountability. Middle managers are hired by the senior managers who should take ownership of middle management results. But the "stink of failure" doesn't get admitted until the middle guys are pressured to do something, leave, or are forced out. The really good people see this happening around them and leave well in advance of the impending storm. The act of making middle management changes translates as "tough" senior management in press releases. The public markets tend to applaud this new toughness (they love the word "ouster") and gives the company another temporary pass. So this ploy can be effective for a time.

The end game of the process is when things don't turn around after all the trumpeted "improvements." The senior guys are now on the hot seat. The next predictable moves are announcements about a change of "strategy," and trying to reach "new markets." This if often accompanied by a radical organizational change. In other words, the entire game plan, sometimes even the name of the game, for the entire company or organization must change to protect the guys at the top.

But pay attention here. Who has been making all of the decisions all along? Who was making the decisions as the company went into distress? Well, that would be senior management. Who made the wrong hiring and staffing decisions? Well, that would be senior management. Who had the wrong strategy or the wrong plan? Again, that would be senior management. My question is: Why not look to senior management first when things start to tank? If they are left in place, is it really logical to think those guys will get it right the second time around?

It seems pretty straightforward that the fundamental problems at all enterprises are almost always at the top of the organizational chart. The secretaries and janitors aren't killing businesses. Like trees, they die from the top down.

24

REARRANGING DECK CHAIRS ON THE TITANIC

The phrase above creates a powerful image of doing something totally futile in the face of complete devastation and failure. It is an exaggerated image to be sure. But, it captures one of the classic and common failings in business. It is critical to address situations before the business "ship" actually hits an "iceberg." Frenetic change for the sake of change after the fact is more akin to the scurrying around that happens after the ship is taking on water, and inclined to portend a fatal outcome.

Of course, this is the situation that consultants encounter all the time. Organizations and executives aren't typically seeking out fundamental change to address challenges and unexpected obstacles – even the ones that are obvious and have disastrous consequences. Fundamental change is hard to do. Fundamental change means that the decisions made in the past are suspect. Fundamental change needs support from other parts of an organization, especially from above.

Fundamental change may be risky for one's career. There is tremendous resistance to engage in any activity that is hard and risky. So consultants may be called in to provide "band aid" type advice, often to a deeply-rooted direction that puts an entire organization in the path of an iceberg.

If the captain of the Titanic knew he was going to hit the iceberg do you think he would have slowed the ship down, waited for daylight, or altered his course? We certainly would have done this as rational people and leaders in the face of certain evidence of failure – wouldn't we? And yet, the world is full of ships, icebergs and incompetent seamanship.

Here are the signs to become aware of on your watch. When the solution to every organizational problem is to restructure, over and over again, then you have a clue that you are in dangerous waters. Constant restructuring is almost always a sign of organizational ineptitude and the figurative lack of either a map or a compass. Once you have the proper charts and tools (this is the hard part) then you can justify one, last, fundamental reorganization to focus the team on a shared purpose and measurable goals. Here is where consultants can be most valuable. I'm not speaking about the type that charge large fees, put newly-minted MBAs on the case, and then delivers another piece of "shelf ware." No, I'm talking about the kind of consultant that has "been there." They understand that the organization is in need of direction and they will be a catalyst to engender the sense of urgency into the process of avoiding the iceberg.

Another sign to watch is when there is a revolving door of middle management within an organization. This signals that the people on the top aren't really committed to avoiding the iceberg. The people on the bottom are clueless about what the possible iceberg might mean to them and they are comfortable being clueless. The folks in the middle clearly see what is happening. Did the owners of the White Star Line really think much about icebergs? They were concerned with making a fast passage and touting their unsinkable ship. Were the passengers on the Titanic even mindful of the dangers of icebergs? I doubt it. The captain and crew were placed in the untenable position between senior management and passengers. It must have been the worst possible nightmare for all of them, and ultimately it had consequences for everyone concerned.

What seems to happen in business practice is that the smart and committed junior leaders that are needed to energize an organization are the first to really "get it." These individuals make career changes when things start to feel frustrating and futile at work, and when there is grave concern about the future. Figuratively, they are heading for the lifeboats ahead of all the other passengers on the boat. When this starts to happen it is time to either 1) change the course of the business, if you can, or 2) make plans for your own safe passage away from the boat.

The saddest of all scenarios is when the business or organization is actually doomed, much like the Titanic, but all the people on the boat are in denial. When a boat sinks, it takes down lots of innocents. Think of Enron and all those folks with their retirements attached to company stock. If you are headed for an iceberg or on a sinking boat, you must make immediate plans for survival. There is no point to trying to "rearrange the deck chairs."

25

Good managers know the rules —

Great managers know the exceptions

This adage is so straightforward that you would think that it would be hard for a good manager to make mistakes. But it happens all the time. There are actually two different components to the adage, sides of the same coin if you will. Yet, there is an inherent tendency to ignore one side at the expense of the other side.

The starting point must be for the manager to actually know the rules. Some rules are matters of law and should be well known by all. But many rules are unique to the individual business or enterprise. These can be written or unwritten. They can be formal, informal or cultural (like allowing excused days for religious holidays). But, the rules are always there to remind a manager of what is considered to be good business practice, in the best interest of a successful organization. So, there are rules for accounting, rules for shareholder reporting, rules for employee conduct and rules that guide the responsibilities of individuals within an organization. Some of these are codified into employee manuals. Some are passed along as oral tradition. It is incumbent on a person to care enough to know the rules within an organization. Moreover, it is imperative for the people in an organization to respect and follow those rules. Good managers need to hold employees to high standards. Rules are part of maintaining high standards.

There are two classic abuses to living by the rules. The first is to hold fast to a rule at the expense of common sense, especially when the interests of the company are better served by circumventing the rule. I was exposed to a classic violation of this type just recently. A large corporation with a new product line sold a sizable order to a new and equally sizable customer. When the product was delivered, it was deemed by the customer (and any logical person looking in from the outside) to be deficient against the promised performance. In order to fix the problem and deliver the product up to specifications, some additional re-work had to be done. When this was finished, the division of the company doing the re-work (ironically, the same one that created the deficient product in the first instance) billed the new customer for additional work. This drove the customer into a tirade. This message was delivered to the original sales person who had the client relationship. Looking for relief, the sales person petitioned his division head that the work should be done at no expense to the customer. The division head responded that all additional work must be billed out. It was the rule. Not finding a sympathetic ear, the sales person petitioned his case higher. Again, the rules of the company didn't allow for any free work. In exasperation the sales person, with his immediate line manager's consent, created a bogus internal account that could be billed for internal work, and mailed a rebate check back to the customer. When this was discovered by the accounting department, all hell broke loose. Why? Because, this was against the internal accounting rules of the company.

The solution should have been to acknowledge the product deficiency and make the customer "whole" from the get go – perhaps with an apology. There may not be rules for such action, but clearly it was called for. Someone in management should have made an exception. Why jeopardize an entire customer relationship over some internal rule or petty territorial squabble? It isn't worth it.

Of course, there are organizations where the rules are fiction and everything is managed by exception. This abuse, the other side of the coin, can be just as dangerous to the long-term health of the enterprise. It may be more dangerous. So, the adage about exceptions shouldn't be used with frequency to justify decisions that are capricious. The rules exist for a reason. If you don't like a rule and find yourself always trying to circumvent it, the proper course of action is to attempt to have the rule changed. Then there will be a new rule. If you find that you are always managing by exception, take a good look at your rules. They may deficient. Of course, the alternate conclusion could be that you may also have management issues.

The greatest managers know the rules, they know the exceptions and they know that exceptions aren't the rule.

26

THERE ARE NO
SILVER MEDALS IN BUSINESS

We've all become accustomed to thinking patterns that are quite contrary to actual business practice. It is difficult to reprogram ourselves from outdated and incorrect thinking into a new and better thought processes that we need to embrace for success.

One clear example: business is not like school, where there are rewards for second place – or third place, or for "participation." We have been conditioned by our years of school experiences, where it is probably unfair and unwise to pick a single winner, leaving everyone else as losers. This would be very hard on the fragile egos and the self-esteem of children. They are adult WIP (work in process) and must be cherished. Far be it from me to suggest a fundamental change in the way we mold our children into contributing adults. It is the fortunate child that actually has someone on their side who cares about their development and future success. I wouldn't change any of this. But the closest we get to business reality in youth development is in athletics, where in the end there is at least a team winner and a team loser (even if everyone gets trophies).

This reward and recognition model continues into higher education. It is reasonable for a student to not panic over the difference between an "A" and a "B." Never mind that there is tremendous grade inflation at all levels and in all institutions. At the end of the day, it really doesn't matter. How many times have you heard a student say: "Nobody ever asks you what your grades were anyway? All they care about is whether or not you graduated." To some degree they are right. It might come as a surprise to highly competitive graduate programs, top law schools, and all medical schools that this thinking exists. These programs tend to only see student applicants with their "motors" on high. The thinking even creeps into the educator side of the equation where grades are dispensed like candy. Parents are also very inclined to believe the thinking that: "Standardized tests really don't matter and don't measure the complete person." Of course they don't. But, *they do measure something.* And in a vacuum, that measurement matters. But I digress.

So, when they finally land into a competitive business situation, young adults are unprepared for the rules of the game. Business is simple. It has A and B answers. In other words, it is bifurcated. There is no overlap, and usually very little grey area, between two possible outcomes. *There are no silver medals.* There are no trophies that get distributed to the players that made every practice. There are no grade point averages to worry about. There is just a series of bifurcated events, with real winners and losers.

On the simplest scale, it starts early in the business world. You either get the job or you don't. There are no accolades for being the first runner up, unless the winner decides not to take the job. Promotions are the same way. There may be a field of good candidates, but generally only one person gets the position. The others don't. Many ugly internal work situations are fueled by the inability of the losers to adjust to this reality and then carry on.

When you are in sales you are confronting this bifurcated world hour by hour, day by day. One of the great disconnects in business is that the sales team has constantly to live with this straightforward, but brutal, set of rules – while the remainder of the organization maybe allowed to wallow in and out of the cozy world of theory. There is a continuation of the education model that some organizations embrace as their "culture." When you're a sales person, you either make the sale or you don't. Rare is the case when after a sale is lost the customer has pity on the loser and then buys a smaller amount than the winner's share. That would be bad business. As consumers we understand this bifurcated point clearly. We can only buy one. So, we buy the one we think is best.

CEOs, especially those of public companies, have another layer of reality. Either the company is doing better, or it isn't. The stock price is up, or it is down. Keeping one's job is highly correlated to positive news, and the absence of good news makes one's position highly vulnerable. You don't get demoted down a rank or get to sit-out a few games. You are out.

The lesson here is that business is not like school. There are no silver medals. Get used to it and embrace the fundamental difference. Then always shoot for the gold.

27

THERE ARE NO SILVER BULLETS

There are numerous delusions in business. The notion that there will be an event of unexpected good fortune that will save an otherwise doomed project or enterprise is at the top of the list.

There are many ways to say this. I've chosen an easy one to remember. *There are no silver bullets.* This is a reference to my childhood television viewing where the *Lone Ranger* was so special that he had only silver bullets instead of the customary copper or lead. As the symbol for good overcoming evil, it was rare that the Lone Ranger had to fire his gun. But when he did, the fortunes of those wearing the "white hats," the good guys in other words, were made secure.

You could just as easily say that in business there is no Santa Claus or Tooth Fairy. They would be equally accurate statements in capturing this very same concept. Consider the practical variation that commonly occurs within families. There's the belief that "things will change when long-lost Uncle Bill leaves us a fortune."

This may be bad for Uncle Bill, but good for the heirs. Never mind that one's personal actions and those of Uncle Bill are separate and distinct - both before and after his demise. A friend of mine refers to this as variation as the "lucky sperm" delusion.

If it is so obvious that there are no silver bullets in business, why do managers believe in the power of the unexpected positive event? The reasons are simple. First, every once in a while lightning actually hits and a business or project is saved from doom by shear dumb luck. How many times have you heard the adage "it is better to be lucky than good?" Business people are inherently optimistic and so they talk themselves into believing that if they stay at it long enough something good is bound to happen. Another version of the same thought: "Even a blind squirrel finds a nut once in a while."

The other reason for the popularity in believing in silver bullets is that on the very rare occasions when some stroke of good fortune actually materializes, legends are created. You usually find little mention of business failures. But the successes attributed to dumb luck are broadcast far and wide. It isn't too hard to be convinced that something good could happen to you. Pick up a newspaper on any given day for proof. I'll bet there is some story about a little old lady in Kansas finding a Lincoln photograph in her attic, or that of a potato chip in the shape of Idaho which sold on EBay for a small fortune.

The truth is that luck (if we are to acknowledge the presence of a random force completely divorced from the reality of hard work) is fickle. The simplest concept is "Heads you win. Tails you lose." There is a 50-50 chance of luck being on your side. If it were this simple we might be more inclined to believe in the Tooth Fairy. Unfortunately for the instincts of a manager turned gambler, the fundamental equations of complex businesses always have more than one variable. Expanding the set of outcomes exponentially creates an equation with a mathematically low probability. A number of key factors would all have to simultaneously align to create a stupendously lucky event. But once in a while it does happen. And the legend continues.

Of course, the other fallacy in this thinking is that even if good luck were to descend upon a business, the magnitude of the "luck" would need to be so large as actually to change the course of events permanently. Viewed another way, is the effect of the good luck sustainable? Mathematicians would have a field day with that question. The simple answer for the thinking manager is always "no." Expecting two abnormally lucky events in a row? Nobody is that lucky.

So, how do you play through this delusion? The manager risks being characterized as "negative." Nobody wants to be around people like that, do they? Go back to basics and a simple analysis of how many favorable events would have to occur simultaneously (like stars lining up), or how big one single event would have to be, to make a real difference. Rare is the situation where there is either sufficient quantity or magnitude to make the kind of difference needed to save a business. In the harsh light of day, and with a sober mind, invariably you will come to the unhappy conclusion that there are "no silver bullets."

Delusion time is over. The Lone Ranger is for kids. It is time to start thinking about managing the reality at hand.

28

IF YOU DON'T WANT TO DO IT, OR YOU DON'T HAVE TO DO IT, THEN DON'T DO IT

One of the consistently hot topics on business book-shelves is time management. There are literally scores of books on the subject available at any well-stocked bookstore. Time stress is an area of substantial executive pain. I see it and hear it from my clients. I've experienced it myself. And, to some degree, it never really goes away. So there is a constant appetite to seek some possible relief from any available source.

I'm not the guy with the cure for this "plague" of having too much to do in too little time. I'm sincerely sorry that I'm not because I could make a fortune with the "cure." But, I do have a one-size fits all suggestion that might provide some relief – if you are willing to swallow a little "medicine."

The advice is in the title above. If you don't want to do something, and/or you don't have to do something, then just don't do it. Say no. Significant opportunities for time saving fall within this advice umbrella, both in business and in our personal lives. Once you start using this simple yardstick your decisions are often easier to make.

Of course, so much responsibility while engaged in a business or organization is considered "must carry" baggage. There are expectations and assignments that are genuinely unpleasant for executives. But they must be done. So, these fall into an easy category to understand – *must do*. The notion of retirement is often framed as the absence of having to do these types of unpleasant tasks. Most executives I know would never retire if they thought they could cherry-pick the interesting and rewarding parts of their current jobs, and assign the "dreck" to someone else. But that isn't realistic. So you must accept the whole enchilada or walk away from it. I've heard more than my share of executives frame their decisions to quit in just those terms – they finally have "walking away money."

But, it would be truthful to make the observation that many executive tasks aren't really "must dos," and could be ignored or dispensed with. Be alert and pay attention. Here is where the sweet spot is, both at your job and at home. Some activities have a life of their own through inertia and repetition. But, they may not deserve to live at all.

For example, business travel is one of the repeat offenders which often present enormous opportunities for time management. And it cuts both ways. Some travel is superfluous and done just to "wave the flag." I know executives that think by traveling they are proving to the organization that they are busy and indispensable. But are all the meetings really necessary? Or, can meetings with as much impact be accomplished over the telephone?

However, there are some activities that are best and most efficiently accomplished face to face, especially those between a manager and a reporting line. You must be there to project forcefulness with your body language and to observe the body language of others. I see as many managers making dumb trips as I see managers not making smart trips. Start with travel, and work your way into self-analysis of many of the activities and policies that control your life. If you don't want to do these, and you don't need to do them, then stop.

I had a personal experience that may help illustrate the point. After some coaxing by a friend, I allowed my name to be submitted to serve on one of the volunteer boards in my small New England town. I thought it would be fun. And I thought I'd be serving my community, which should be a good thing. After only a few months, the tenor of this volunteer job became apparent. The board wasn't really committed to taking the unpopular positions necessary to improve the town, although a minority of the members was. The public meetings evolved into tension-filled sessions of steady confrontation between the lax status quo members and those of us that felt a responsibility to serve with a serious agenda. At one critical time, it also became obvious that the Selectmen (our highest board of elected officials) really didn't want to endure the pain of progress and leaned in the direction of the status quo. I came home from a number of meetings totally frustrated and angry. That's when it occurred to me to follow this advice. So, I resigned. Now I'm much happier on Tuesday evenings, twice every month. Maybe the town is less well-served. They may not care. Me either. A good time management decision was made.

29

ONLY THREE THINGS
ARE IMPOSSIBLE

There are only three things that are impossible. The list is presented below, with appropriate clarification. But the central point is that most things you think about attempting in business and life aren't really impossible. True, they may be difficult. Yes, they may stretch your talents and resources to the breaking point. But that doesn't render them impossible. So, keep your objectives lofty, your goals aggressive and your standards high. Now for the list.

1) ***Dribbling a football is impossible.*** Give it a try, and you'll agree. The point of mentioning this is that there are actually lots of tasks that are physically impossible. It is the wise person that doesn't delude himself or herself into thinking that they can change and overcome the inherent laws of science, mathematics or nature. It just won't happen. Ergo, impossible.

2) ***Unscrambling an egg is impossible***. There is no way to even attempt to do this in the kitchen, so why assume you can do this in an organization. The key feature to remember here is that once you mix all the ingredients of a deal or a collective working group of people

together for any amount of time, the bad or dysfunctional properties of the resulting recipe cannot be extracted successfully. The most viable path is to throw the figurative "entrée" away and start from scratch. The whole lot has to be scrapped – something which is hard to do. So lots of time and effort gets expended on attempting this trick – which is impossible.

3) ***Dressing a baby with one hand is impossible.*** Please don't even attempt to do this as a way of proving me wrong. Value your children. What is the business cor ollary to this exception? Simply this - nothing in business, commerce or organizations actually happens with only one person doing all the work. At the very least a single transaction involves two parties. No one-handed dressing here. But more often than not, real success takes many people in the mix. There are teams of inventors, customers, marketers, accountants, manufacturers. The list grows quite quickly. So, as a man ager it is important to stop acting as if you can dress a baby with one hand. Again, impossible.

For all the other myriad of opportunities and challenges you might face, attack them boldly with creativity, hard work and common sense. Really, only three things are impossible!

30

IF YOU KNEW
YOU WOULDN'T FAIL,
WHAT WOULD YOU DO?

I read a magazine article that started with this question many years ago. I wish I could provide the source. This "master question" raises an interesting and complex cascade of possibilities for businesses, organizations and our own personal lives.

Brainstorming can be an invigorating process. So, start there. What would you actually do knowing that you would not fail? Write everything down. My guess is that this isn't a list that comes easily. I don't know if this is because our minds start channeling the thought impulses in directions that unconsciously protect us from going down the wrong roads. Or perhaps the question is really daunting. It is like being given a blank white canvas and paints a set of and then being told that whatever was painted would be a "masterpiece." Now, what to do? If you actually get a list on paper (which I encourage you to try), the exercise still isn't over. The process must continue, for it to be useful.

Give your list the "once over" against the adage that "only three things are impossible" (see Chapter 29).

This is because impossibility preempts failure. Some things are impossible to accomplish – defying the laws of nature, internally changing the toxic behavior of sick organizations and accomplishing something great totally on your own, without others. Edit your list against these caveats and now there will be the start of a useful roadmap.

Now, ask yourself, how committed would you be to actually achieving any one of the goals on your list? Your list undoubtedly gets more focused in this process. Lots of our "wishes" really are unrealistic and not tethered to our own powers of concentration and accomplishment – like "I want to win the lottery." Eliminate these from the list.

Having completed this, there probably aren't all that many items left that you would really want to do if you knew you wouldn't fail. No matter how many there are, it is probably unrealistic to think you can do them all. This is where I personally get bogged-down. I see many things I'd like to do, and they all still look relatively achievable (like writing a book someday). Perhaps this could be called the "Renaissance Man" complex. I'm not the only person that suffers from this.

Once the list is pared-down to a handful of possible goals, the time has come to pick one to which you would apply maximum effort to achieve, at the complete exclusion of the others (at least for a time). Now, try putting a plan together to actually achieve the goal. The purpose of the plan is to break the process into incremental parts, baby steps if you will, to begin marching forward toward the goal.

When you follow this process, you might be surprised to discover that you may have already cleared most of the hurdles that doom "ideas" from becoming "achievements." It doesn't mean that you won't fail.

But the powers of ingenuity and concentration are a hard combination of factors to discount when viewed against goals that aren't inherently impossible. You can do it.

The only factor that might stop you now is your fear. Once you realize this, you are liberated because success of some degree is guaranteed.

Section V
PLANNING WISE

31

PEOPLE DON'T PLAN TO FAIL, THEY SIMPLY FAIL TO PLAN

You may have already spotted one of the recurring themes of this book. It is the importance of having a plan – or even better, having a good plan.

Here is the unfortunate truth. Enough people succeed in business and life without well-thought-out plans that it is quite seductive to attempt working without one. However, this only acknowledges a certain randomness to life. People win the lottery too. And their only planning is to buy a lottery ticket. People inherit money with no plan at all, except perhaps for staying on the good side of Aunt Millie. People get promoted in family businesses because they are, well, family (no planning required). It must also be acknowledged that random events also dispense bad outcomes, sometimes even when there is a good plan.

Holding freakish, random events aside, success almost always requires a plan. The degree of success is highly correlated to the quality and detail of the plan. So, if you aren't trying to fail, all the planning you do should be helpful. That's the premise.

The question is: Does planning really work? As business practitioners, we'd instinctively like to believe that it does. In fact, usually it does. What does seem to be absolute is that failure to plan is tantamount to statistically risking failure. At least we should agree that putting together a plan is a safe bet. It can't hurt any.

The real issue with plans is the quality of the plan. Good plans are more effective than bad plans. Bad plans are still much better than no plans at all. To illustrate this I'm reminded of a story from my own family.

Many years ago a fifteen-year-old cousin of mine ran off with her high school boyfriend, reportedly headed for Florida. My aunt and uncle were terrified. After a couple of days without news from the police around this missing person case, my aunt decided she needed to do something. She put together a plan – one that everyone in the family thought was not very well thought out. In fact, we all thought it was absurd. She decided to go to Florida and sit by the entrance to Disney World until her daughter showed up. The Disney people couldn't have been nicer about the situation and found a place for her to park her lawn chair near the entrance and in the shade. My aunt sat there every day for over two weeks, watching thousands of people enter the Magic Kingdom. Finally she was rewarded when my cousin and her boyfriend tried to enter the park. This is a true story. It demonstrates the power of a plan, even one that appeared flawed.

Good plans have common elements. They are very *specific* about the goal targeted to be achieved. They are *realistic* to the degree that the goal can be achieved without divine intervention. They are better if they are *simple* – it makes them easier to understand and communicate to others, especially if others are required to assist. They are *time-bound,* with a target date for achievement and milestones along the way to mark progress toward the goal. They have *specific tasks* assigned to specific people, and those people are held *accountable* for executing their part of the plan. As part of the planning process it is also important to *monitor progress* and *adjust the plan* as necessary to achieve the goals.

Looking back on it, I'm not sure that my aunt didn't get it mostly right, even if her plan was an instinctive reaction forced by sheer terror. She was very specific in what she was trying to do – find her daughter (using means that had to be unconventional, because conventional means weren't working). The plan was realistic. She could do it herself with limited financial resources and unlimited time. It was time-bound to some extent. She believed that two teenagers from New England wouldn't be able to occupy themselves very long without going to the biggest attraction in the state. She had a specific task, and enlisted others to help her. She was personally accountable and literally sat every day, all day, until her daughter arrived. I can only imagine her relief when she finally saw her daughter approaching the entrance gate. I suspect the understandable anger came later.

In fact, looking back I'd have to give my aunt lots of credit for inventing a workable plan in a situation where it must have been difficult even imaging a plan of action. If you knew my aunt, you would know that she wasn't planning to fail.

32

How does the movie end?

I work with many clients, all trying to build or improve their businesses. After I get to know them a little (so they won't think I'm impertinent), I always ask them the same question: "How does the movie end?" More often than not I get a puzzled look, the knit forehead and a question back in return. "What do you mean?"

I mean, how does the movie, your personal or company movie, end? How does this drama you are involved with that we call an enterprise come to some conclusion? Of course, this leads to the kinds of conversations that are really important in business – conversations about horizons, goals, strategies and plans. Truthfully, very few business executives view their engagements as part of a movie with a beginning, middle and an ending – with multiple plots to be written in between.

Moreover, executives usually never see the movie as ending. Be forewarned, the movie or one's time on the business stage always ends. It is hard to imagine that the people officially watching the movie (investors, shareholders, directors and key employees) view the drama in anything less than finite terms. In this day and age, it is difficult to imagine the business movie lasting more than five years. The audience becomes fatigued. Many companies now do their planning in three-year cycles to acknowledge the rapid changes in their respective industries.

So, start by admitting to yourself that the current business you are leading actually ends (as it is known today) in five years – at the most. How do you want the results to look five years out when the reviews start pouring in?

By this point in the conversation my clients are quite sober and are facing the reality of having to formulate plans that really work. This is because ultimately the ending will be either a happy one or a disappointing one. The executive needs to take charge of the ending.

If you can paint a picture of how you would like the movie to end, you are in a much better position to write the plot to get there. The intermediate goals and actions that are necessary to deliver the required results are brought into much sharper focus. The matters that are extraneous to the plot are also easier to identify and much easier to ignore. They don't contribute much to the ending.

The biggest benefit to this kind of thinking is that you are much more aware of the value and passage of time. The ability to achieve the goal is defined by the time allowed. The movie will end in about five years (maybe less) whether you are on your game or not. A sense of urgency will collapse time frames for action, make hard decisions easier to make, and bring a group of trusted confidants closer together in the face of the impending end.

Remember, while all movies end, there are often sequels to the really good ones. This is the longer term view. But, don't kid yourself into thinking that you are really managing for the long term and that the forces around you "don't really get it" because they are demanding short-term results. This is the lame thinking of academics, family-owned businesses and self-serving executives that have lost their fastballs (so to speak). The brutal truth is that we are all constantly measured in relatively short time frames. We must deliver. If we do, then someone is probably going to invite us to be part of the sequel, or perhaps a brand new movie, maybe one even bigger and better than the first.

So, what do my clients eventually do with my question? A couple have been sufficiently un-nerved by it that they terminate the relationship after a short but cordial relationship. These are the guys that really don't want to live in a world of urgency, plans and measured results. I'm better off without the frustrations of living in their world.

Fortunately, most of the executives do "get it" and they become very focused on what their respective roles are and what needs to be done toward writing a successful script. They are a pleasure for a consultant to work with. They don't want slide shows and books to store on the shelf. They want to roll up their sleeves get working. They are the kind of clients that somebody might decide to make a movie about!

33

IDEAS ARE EITHER PRICELESS OR WORTHLESS

I would be a wealthy man if I had a dime for every time someone has said to me: "I have an idea for you." I've actually come to resent people who constantly do this. And, I abhor the person that believes they have been anointed as "the idea person" while the rest of us are expected to salute their self-appointed superior status.

I've come to realize that ideas are either priceless or worthless. What defines the difference are the additional steps of formulating a plan for achieving the potential of an idea and then executing the plan to successful completion. Doing this is extremely hard work. The individuals that can put an idea together with a successful result are unusual and special. Executives are called upon to be those people.

I'll admit it, I'm all for creative group thinking and brainstorming. It is a useful technique to get individuals and groups moving toward a shared result. Part of the process is to withhold judgments on the efficacy of the ideas. I like participating in this process, especially with creative people. It is stimulating and fun. But even after an organized process, the ideas really shouldn't be valued beyond the "worthless" category unless the process of brainstorming extends further into the planning and execution phases.

Almost all ideas are worthless, right off the bat. They aren't practical. They are incomplete in their formation. They have no context. Perhaps they have the added disadvantage of being self-serving from the outset. Most of what the so-called "idea people" dispense is absolute drivel. Yet, as a society, we have elevated ideas up onto a pedestal. So, weak and thoughtless people attempt to raise their own stature by elevating their ideas in public. It wouldn't make me so angry if they actually attempted, eventually, to do something. But, like bees, they buzz off to the next flower to share their new ideas somewhere else.

Idea people can fast become disruptive and counter-productive to something of value being accomplished. A good venue to observe this behavior is on a charitable board or committee, where everyone is volunteering their time and it isn't appropriate to neglect contributions of any kind (lest they be attached to some money). Other more explicit situations to observe the behavior are the small business owned by an individual, or the new business driven by founders that view themselves as savants. The ideas, like Top 40 radio hits, "just keep on coming." This can be so overwhelming that line managers assigned with achieving day-to-day results never really know what to do next. Is it right to follow the original plan? Or, is it right to follow the latest tangent that the boss inserts into the process? In cases like these ideas are beyond worthless, they are destructive.

To make ideas priceless requires two forces that act as counterweights against each other (think of a see-saw). The first force is *idea police*. Eventually, all ideas need to be evaluated, including the ones that are the product of organized brainstorming. Getting this done sooner, rather than later, is one of the primary tasks of responsible management. You don't have to be the person thinking the big thoughts to be an outstanding manager. But, you do have to be the person that can quickly triage incoming ideas and then boil things down into the next steps a team needs to move forward.

The second force is the *idea champion*. If the idea is to become priceless it first needs to clear the idea police's evaluation criteria. Then it must have at least one person committed to realizing the idea – a champion. I have enormous respect for anyone that drops an idea into a conversation, like a live grenade, and then falls on it with the determined commitment to get it done.

Allow me to tell you a personal story to illustrate the point. When my son was a medical student he thought it would be a great idea to organize an alumni group at his university for the generations of graduates who had gone on to become doctors. This school did not have its own medical school and therefore had no internal mechanism to organize its alumni, over 10% of whom are physicians. After doing market research (which acted as the idea police) he concluded it was a good idea. But (ever the parent), I pointed out that the idea was either priceless or worthless. It depended on a viable plan and my son's commitment to execute it. Much to my pleasure, and somewhat to my surprise, my son really took hold of planning and executing his idea. After three years (as of this writing) there are over 1300 doctors as members in this new alumni group. A number of well-intentioned members have claimed that they had the idea for a similar group many years earlier. This has happened so many times as to become pleasantly humorous to my son and me. Now he gets it.

He has benefited from an unforgettable life lesson. I have had the satisfaction of playing the father-role one more time. This truly makes his idea priceless to me.

34

"IF YOU'RE NOT ON BROADWAY, YOU'RE OUT OF TOWN."

This is a quote that I believe is attributed to George M. Cohen, the Broadway impresario and legend. In the New York theatre culture there is a distinct line of demarcation between "Broadway" and "Out of Town." The essence of the quote is that to be considered serious you must prove your worth at the highest level, to a very limited and definable peer group. Failing to make it in the "big leagues" is the equivalent of an absolute failure, because the big leagues are all that really matter.

As with many of the topics I write about, there is a tendency for individuals and companies to be delusional about their true position in the marketplace or their prospects for future success. This delusion can be a barrier to actually finding a market niche or making slight adjustments to formulate a plan that could lead to alternative success. In other words, it is always a good idea to know where "Broadway" is. Then add to this knowing if you are there, or how far away it is if you are not there.

For example, I've had the opportunity to see lots of start-up technologies that require massive distribution to be successful. We're talking millions of units. Typically, these are companies offering some added feature to available software or they have imbedded middleware that must be packed with a new computer. The easiest case to understand is security software that needs to be loaded onto the hard drive of new computers to achieve mass distribution and success. There are at least two major hurdles to accomplishing this. First, the product must be special and good enough to attract the interest of the computer OEMs (Original Equipment Manufacturers) to justify placement on their units, and presumably give them a competitive advantage. The second issue is pricing. Computer OEMs are so pressed to provide competitive pricing in the marketplace that they resist adding additional "cents" to the cost of their units. In fact, they view their distribution network as a profit center. You might be able to get software planted on the unit (the typical trials of anti-virus software for example) but you have to pay the OEMs for this privilege. Doing this has the effect of actually lowering the manufactured cost of the computer "in the box" and provides a larger profit margin to the OEM.

In the environment I'm describing above, being "on Broadway" means being inserted in the box by the OEM. Any other plan for distribution is "Out of Town."

This chapter is obliquely about understanding and overcoming dependencies. You can't ignore them or pretend they don't exist just because they are inconvenient. You have to appreciate them, work through them, work around them or understand that they are informing you that a path to success is forever closed.

If you want to become a doctor and practice in the United States you must have a medical license. But, to follow this illustrative example, there are many other dependencies along the way. You must attend college – and moreover you must survive rigorous science courses, like the dreaded Organic Chemistry. You must get into medical school and graduate, no trivial task. You must get placed into a residency program to even qualify to take the medical board exams. For someone with the aspirations of becoming a doctor, these dependencies are eventually understood and integrated into their plan.

When my son started his freshman year, about 40% of his incoming college class designated "Pre-med" as their career goal – more than 800 young men and women. When graduation rolled around, slightly more than 200 were actually accepted at a medical or a dental school. This is a large number, but it represents only 25% of the original group. What happened along the way? Some voluntarily changed their minds for sure, but probably no more than those that started in other majors and decided they wanted to become doctors, substitution in the reverse direction. The falloff was a direct result of dependencies and not being able, or willing, to overcome them. My son related the story of the advanced chemistry professor that welcomed the class on the first day with the words: "For some of you this is the first step toward a profession in medicine, for others of you this will be a course in pre-Business."

Without knowing it, that professor was providing modern-day confirmation that George M. Cohen had it right. "If you're not on Broadway, you're Out of Town."

35

THERE ISN'T MUCH DIFFERENCE BETWEEN THE "LEADING EDGE" AND THE "BLEEDING EDGE"

This chapter is written for start-up companies focused on new and emerging technologies. With that as introduction, the title is almost self-explanatory if you are engaged in the process.

I've had the opportunity to look at business plans for scores of technology, Internet and so-called "dot-com" businesses in the past decade. Almost all of them were looking for investment capital and my job was to analyze the potential return on a possible investment in the company.

At this point, a little background may be instructive. There has been a virtual revolution in communication technology, starting in the mid-1990's. The magnitude of this revolution has probably not been fully appreciated because we have all been part of it and it is far from over as an historical cycle. I was recently involved in a court case and had to put the media environment for 1998 into historical context for a jury that, quite honestly, didn't have a good memory or any handle on what was happening around that time. I told them the story of a couple of guys from Stanford who started a business in June of 1998, in a garage, with a business concept based on their academic work. The product was named Back Rub. With funding of about $1 million later in the same year they were able to successfully launch their business. As of 2005, when I was telling the story, this company had become the most valuable media company on the planet. It still is today. You know it as Google.

Legendary stories about Google, or Yahoo, or eBay or even Microsoft have provided a constant source of fuel to the revolution I've referenced. They were all part of the fabric, but they didn't cause the revolution. This is important to remember. Most of these innovative companies were figuratively "standing on the shoulders of giants" and were beneficiaries of being the right solution to the right problem at the right time. There definitely was a convergence of talent with luck-in-timing. And, there will be even more of that to come. To some degree it resembles a surfer catching the perfect wave.

For perspective, what happened to the fellows who actually invented the electronic computer back in 1949? We don't even remember their names. Or, how about the hand-held calculator called the Bowmar Brain? Most people have never heard of it. Or, what about the people that dreamt of a place to exchange information, which became the Internet. I've read that in 1992, the year Bill Clinton was elected President for his first term, a LexisNexis search for the entire year yields fewer than 1000 entries for the word "Internet." That's for the entire year! Today people think of the Internet as if it has always been there.

Consider, where would the Internet be without guys like Bill McGowan, CEO of MCI? That company boldly invested in fiber optic cables that were dropped into trenches following railroad beds. Today those cables are the backbone of the network that makes the Internet possible.

If you think I'm making a case for the go-go days of investing blindly in technology, you've forgotten the title to this chapter. For every success we can mention there are probably a thousand corporate failures. You see, luck-in-timing is akin to a random event. After it happens it looks planned and inevitable. But when the stars aren't aligned, misplaced timing can inflict cruel punishment on both innovators and investors.

So, my job has become one of trying to put innovative ideas into a context where their viability can be predicted. This is much more difficult than falling in love with a new idea – even one that looks like it will eventually catch on. When the timing is right, you are considered "leading edge." With bad timing, you are "bleeding edge." When bleeding begins, survival strategies must be addressed. Most important among them is that the run-rate of expenses needs to be harnessed to provide enough time for the market to catch up with the success of an inevitable idea.

There is another danger and this one is even harder to judge. Is there another technology (or a couple of guys in a garage somewhere) that will produce better technology and hopscotch over the idea you are evaluating by the time the market catches up? AOL was huge for a while. But they were eclipsed by many providers of connectivity through cheap broadband, which is now ubiquitous in the United States.

Things change with lightning speed in revolutions. Leading and bleeding at the edge aren't very different.

SECTION VI
CUSTOMER WISE

36

RELIEVE SOME KIND OF PAIN

When it comes to providing formal marketing wisdom, or for even defining the term for that matter, there are far too many resources to count. Marketing is a subject with textbooks galore and many experienced and able practitioners. Personally, I am married to a marketing-oriented person, and through her experiences at places like Procter & Gamble and LensCrafters I've learned to assume a humble persona in public. I freely admit that I'm not a marketing expert and I probably won't advance my theoretical knowledge much beyond where I am today.

Truth is, everyone in a managerial capacity must be familiar with some fundamental marketing principles or they are working with an extreme handicap. Just as truthful is the notion that at its core, marketing really isn't rocket science (although some consider it to be non-invasive brain surgery). What are the fundamental truths that should be acknowledged? I can't provide a succinct list. But, I will suggest that a good starting point for any marketing discussion is the following question: "Where is the pain?"

The marketing process begins with the concept that you should be identifying the needs of consumers, either the real ones or the predicted ones. "Where is the pain?" is a good first question to be asking to insure that you are actually on a firm foundation before a marketing strategy and plan can be formulated.

Many times, the executive is brought into the middle of a marketing-driven situation where presumably all the early and necessary groundwork has already been done. From my experience, it would be wrong to make this assumption blindly if you are the person being inserted into the middle of the process. Maybe things are right on track. But, unless you are working with, or for, one of the truly outstanding marketing-oriented companies (and this is a short list) it is not logical to embrace assumptive thinking. Like a house built on a wobbly foundation, the marketing plan without a strong foundation won't "square-up" and provide the strength needed to withstand natural forces that will attack it. So, without being a marketing genius, you may actually be able to disguise yourself as one by asking: "Tell me again, where the pain is that we are addressing?"

The subtext to this question then can be: "Tell me who has this pain, how many of them are there, where do they reside and how much are they willing to pay for pain relief?" There may be real pain out there, or it may be pain that is miscalculated. Somebody might be predicting that there will be pain some day, but they really aren't sure. Or just maybe, this is a cause felt deeply by a few, for pain only felt by a few. The size of the pain usually has to be massive, either in its depth or its breadth, to justify the resources needed to solve it and then yield an attractive payback.

A microcosm for understanding this premise is the pharmaceutical industry. There are too many diseases, conditions and discomforts to enumerate. Pain is virtually everywhere on their radar screens. So, they never really have to search hard to find it. How does a pharmaceutical company decide which pains to address? How would you decide if you were in their position? It makes for an interesting set of questions for you and your business to benchmark against once the marketing process has begun.

There could be ethical and humanitarian reasons for a drug company to continue spending against a project, even if it fails the "size of pain" test. In this industry there are many avenues to reapply and test compounds and formulas as underlying fundamental research.

But, in a nuts and bolts business keeping the losers alive beyond their ability to provide a measurable return on investment isn't sensible. Unfortunately, this is a common practice, generally by fools. Don't be one. Ask the simple question: "Where is the pain?" And, keep asking the question over and over. The answers will point you in the correct direction and away from the pain of failure.

37

FIND OUT WHAT THEY LIKE

My mother, Nancy Hubbard, gets credit for this piece of wisdom. A little background is in order. Through the late 50's and early 60's, my parents made a habit of going to the Shubert Theater in New Haven to see Broadway shows before they went on to their New York runs. Over the years they saw some good shows in this fashion, along with some clunkers I'm sure. To this day my mom lives in her own "musical theatre world" and she has the lyrics of many shows stored in her brain.

One my mother's favorite shows is *Ain't Misbehavin'*. My mom was so tickled by one of that show's songs that she has shared the imbedded wisdom with her adult children. The scene is a brothel and there is a group of new "recruits" seeking guidance from the experienced resident "madame." They are asking a familiar business question: "How do I do my job well?" The answer comes in the form of a musical number. The memorable lyrics to the song are: "Find out what they like, and how they like it. And, give it to them just that way."

I admit this is an unusual source to cite for business advice. But, when my mother related the story she commented that this was pretty good advice to live by generally when you are trying to figure out how to get a job done, provide a service or meet expectations of those around you. The simple advice is to: "Find out what they like." Said another way, "ask them."

Over time I've found countless uses for this simple story. For example, when I've been in the position of trying to determine what customers really want, I've been inclined to go directly to the source with a simple set of questions, either as a substitute for, or in advance of, a complicated outside marketing survey. Or, when I've tried to discover what incentives will work either to attract or energize good people within an organization, again I've discovered that an excellent starting point is to just "ask them."

I believe this approach works because it is disarmingly simple. When you ask a straightforward question, there is a high likelihood that you'll receive an unvarnished, close to the bone, response. There isn't the time for posturing, being clever, or trying to avoid hurting sensitive feelings.

This is a much better technique to apply in person and verbally. This is because in the process of getting the answer, you are also likely to get body language and nuances that would be impossible to get through a phone survey or mail-in questionnaire. And, while this is something akin to a focus group technique, I almost always find that the technique is best applied one-on-one. It is hard to fake one's true feelings when talking to another person. Working one-on-one has the additional benefit of allowing the questioner to probe more deeply around the parts of an answer that are felt with more conviction.

There is an efficiency, a money saving aspect to the approach, which should be obvious. You don't have to get the same strongly felt answer from too many people to have a relatively accurate picture of a widely held sentiment. Even if a full-blown market survey is in order or required, you'll be able to hone-in on the important matters that will merit the time and effort for a detailed answer.

But a good starting point in wanting to find out necessary information – be it from your spouse, from your children, from your employees or from your customers – is to "ask them."

This is just the first step. We aren't yet imagining the possibilities for success that "Giving it to them just that way" might unleash.

38

ONLY ASK RESEARCH QUESTIONS FOR ANSWERS YOU CAN USE

This advice looks so simple on its face. But, I've learned over time that this is one of the most often violated tenets of common sense in market research.

The decision to do research about customers and markets is always a good one. So a manager gets the false sense of security with the decision to proceed. Then the research project is put into the hands of internal staff, or some outside consulting group. On the face of it, this also provides some comfort for the executive making the decision. The research is being conducted by those with the proper training and expertise to do it well. In the hands of experienced professionals there is a good chance for good data.

But sometimes, through a mixture of ineptitude and personal agendas, research is conducted that is expensive, incomplete and just plain wrong. Believe it or not, sometimes the research project is conceived and assembled to achieve inaccurate results. The researchers may not have the proper incentives to arrive at the truth. There may be real incentives to keep the process of evaluation going, or to elicit false and misleading information. In other words, sometimes research projects are "cooked."

The manager commissioning or approving a research project may be completely in the dark about the true veracity of the information or the usefulness of the data in making important decisions. Sometimes they even want to be kept in the dark about the truth. If something fails, then having research that looks legitimate is good cover and may be used to save a career. But, the purpose of this book is not to create "save your hide" scenarios for incompetent executives.

It is far better for an executive to have some idea of what a research project is intended to discover and how it will be conducted. I'm not saying that the executive should lead the project. But he or she should set the tone for the project if it is important. If it isn't important, why do it?

Setting the tone can be done with a simple set of instructions. First, make sure you are addressing the correct audience to obtain the information. Second, keep the time that a respondent needs to spend with the project short. Better answers are delivered in top-of-mind fashion and without user fatigue. And, third, make sure the questions are the right ones.

To achieve point three, while also achieving point two, the questions need to be succinct. Because respondent fatigue can poison the results of a survey after an extended period of time, *don't waste precious time asking questions where the answer is already known, or fairly well understood.* So, what kind of questions should you ask? The best advice is to seek answers to the questions around which actual decisions can be made. The research should be actionable. Keep fine-tuning the really important issues to the point that actual decision making can be done with some degree of reliability. Remember, business is very often a series of bifurcated decisions, go or no-go, upscale or not, value priced or premium priced, basic service or fully "tricked-out." Done well, research should be able to help with decision making that saves money. Remember, you make money when you buy – including buying research.

I had the opportunity to see a research project very early in my career that violated most of the practical advice I'm suggesting. Maybe that's why I'm adamant on the point. A project was conceived by the president of a company. It really was his pet project. Everyone in the organization liked the president, and everyone knew this was his pet project. This was a public company, so there was some degree of accountability that couldn't be ignored. This led to a research project to determine the feasibility of the idea. But, everyone doing the project knew that a study that killed the project would be hard for the CEO to swallow, and possibly detrimental to the career development of the team members identified to make the project a success. So, a very agreeable sample was assembled – one with very different characteristics from those who would actually be called upon to purchase the project with their dollars. The questions could only be described as "soft ball." The answers were almost pre-determined by the way the questions were asked. An expensive research project was conducted by a reputable company which supported the president's vision to proceed. The business plan was implemented and the product was brought to market.

From the first day the project failed to live up to the lofty projections that were made about consumer acceptance, based on the research project projections. After about five years of failed attempts and losses in the millions, the product was eventually abandoned and written off. The conclusion everyone involved had to acknowledge after the third year of frustration was that "the research was faulty." Duh! And, when the project was abandoned, the president actually pointed to faulty research as the reason for failure. Duh, again! Maybe the president really wanted a legitimate research project to be conducted. If he did, he never communicated the proper directions to the people doing the research project. Failure was pre-baked into the process.

Fortunately, I was too young in my career to be affected. But others weren't so fortunate. This is the kind of lesson you never forget.

39

THE THREE MARKETING POSITIONS: BE FIRST. BE BEST. BE DIFFERENT.

It's a little dangerous attempting to simplify a constellation of marketing theories into a litmus test of just three most legitimate marketing positions. I do this knowing that my harshest criticism will be close to home. My wife also went to the Wharton School, majored in marketing, and had a significant career plying her craft with many brilliant minds at Procter & Gamble, LensCrafters and Cincinnati Bell. Serious marketing theoreticians may mock my naiveté. For them, it might be best to move onto another chapter.

But, for the general manager of a division or a business, there is a lot of marketing theory that is tossed about, in part, to make the non-marketing person feel stupid. This creates a need and a dependency for the brilliant marketing minds to weigh in. Sometimes, it is appropriate and necessary. But sometimes it is just plain overkill.

This chapter is about a very simple barometer to use in making judgments about the market viability of a new good or service. We've already talked about identifying "pain" in the marketplace as a good place to start. Once you get beyond that simple check, the next simple test could well be to ask these questions: 1) Is it first to market?, 2) Is it the best product on the market?, 3) Is it different from all the other products in the market in the same category? I've even assigned a point value scale to these questions. I'd say that first is worth 5 points (because almost by definition it is also best because it is alone in the category). Best is worth 3 points. Different is worth 1 point.

What is the power of being first? Well, the most compelling argument is that you are first against a totally untapped market. This means that for a time all the possible customers are yours (a temporary monopoly). This is good. Of course, if something really has market appeal there will be alternatives and competitors in very short order. Still, being first has power. You are able to define the playing field your way. You have high ground to defend against the positioning and the claims of newcomers. For the rest of time you can always define yourself as being the "first," which has considerable cache. But, be careful. Very few ideas are actually so new or distinct as to be first. Rare is the product or service with no competition.

A lot is made of being the best product on the market. But it isn't always the most direct path to success. If you aren't first, then best is obviously the next best thing to be. There will be a higher hurdle to cross for a consumer that knows about the first product, because you have the burden of actually proving you are the best. Sometimes, even doing that isn't enough to get a new product successfully launched and accepted.

A poster child for this dilemma was the battle between VHS and Beta during the 80's when video tape recorders became a household appliance. By most technical measures, Beta, a creation of Sony, was the superior product, by far. Yet, VHS became the standard. Why? This is a little discussed fact, but the porn industry adopted VHS very early in the evolution of video tape because they wanted to be first to market with their low-budget, easy-to-produce product. The major film studios never adopted a standard. So, into this void, Beta never really had a chance. The die was cast because porn had such large market penetration and the early adopters all went to VHS.

When you have to adopt the "different" strategy, it is time to be very careful. This is where most new products land. There is a supposition that there are at least two market competitors. By definition, one was first. And another, again by definition (it may be the same one), is better than the other, or others. Competing for share of mind in the "different" arena is costly and filled with peril. There are likely others, or soon may be others, that need to compete in this exact same market space. The unfortunate reality for product placement is that most retailers and vendors really don't have the shelf or storage space for a broad range of products in the same category. The other unfortunate reality is that most consumers don't really do well with complicated choices in the marketplace, especially when there are three or more almost-equal alternatives. Making a living on the "different square" of the marketing game board is exceedingly challenging.

Then there is a tendency to think of "cheaper" as one way to be different. I suppose that is valid with a product that is exactly the same in every dimension (like gasoline). But, in general, "cheaper" is not a viable long-term strategy for a market product that hasn't already turned into a commodity. Being cheaper only puts temporary pressure on the folks that are first, best or somehow different to lower their prices to meet the competition. There is always the danger that one of these guys will actually try to re-position the "cheaper" player as also being short on quality. Being known as the "low quality" product is a loser.

40

MARKET TO THE MASSES
AND LIVE WITH THE CLASSES
(AND VICE-VERSA)

I have to thank my friend Nelson Schwab for introducing me to this adage. Nelson ran the theme park division of the former Taft Broadcasting when we both worked there. If ever there was a business designed to market to the masses, theme parks would be front and center.

The underlying concept behind this adage is what I call "the law of large numbers." If there is a product that can be sold to hundreds of thousands, even millions, of consumers there is a good chance that meaningful profit can be made. Even the smallest profit margins generate large gross profit numbers with the multiplier effect of mass consumption. Add a little pricing power to the equation (theme parks, professional sports and cable television are prime industries that have played this game consistently) and the power of the masses explodes. Control expenses and efficiently manage a business that fits this profile and you have the formula for living with the "classes." The interesting thing about the "classes" is they don't much care where you get your money, just that you have money.

It is interesting is to study the inverse of the above adage. If you market to the classes, you may end up living with the masses. Allow me to make the comment that there is absolutely nothing inferior about living with the masses - especially in America, where we all have access to opportunities for education, health and well being. In the historical sense, all of us are living with the classes, with life styles that would have been the envy of the wealthiest only one hundred years ago.

But the adage goes a little deeper, into a "law of small numbers" if you will. Simply stated, there are many businesses that don't have many possible customers. Luxury items are so expensive that only a very small sliver of society can afford to consume them (think private aircraft, yachts, expensive collectibles, etc.). Oftentimes, with such consumables there are too many goods chasing too few qualified customers. Pricing power is diminished and margins shrink. The businesses that are tied to the very richest customers can be risky in terms of consistency of cash flow. The net effect is that, except for the cleverest sales approach or semi-monopolist enterprises, the chances of making large profits are skewed against that possibility. There just aren't enough customers and enough sustainable customer flow to guarantee long-term business success.

One of the variations on this theme, that is an exception of sorts, is that the business of brokering expensive items between wealthy individuals can be a very good business. The primary reason is that the same inventory can be bought and sold many times (like artwork, or high-end real estate). It doesn't mean that the ultimate seller always makes a profit, but the middle man always does because it is formula driven with a commission schedule. The brokerage business has attractive attributes if it qualifies as a good "meter drop" business (see Chapter 49).

Living with the classes requires selling to the masses. You might raise the question of inherited money. Plenty of people living with the classes wouldn't know how to start or run a business. True enough. But somewhere in their family history there was a forbearer who applied the rule. I guarantee it.

41

SELLING IS LIKE BASEBALL

This chapter could easily be the longest one in the book. I've used this metaphor in many settings, from trying to describe quickly the sale process to a novice to complete two-day seminars on the subject to experienced sales teams. I've never known anyone to dissect the process in quite the same way. But the notion of dividing the sales process into workable pieces isn't new. That is precisely the point.

Selling is a numbers game. You can't have any more paying customers than you start with as legitimate target customers. It is unlikely that you'll have 100% sales success, so there is inherent fall-off in the selling process. Over time, and for industry or market segments, there emerges a predictable rate of sales success. Often you hear sales managers predict that a good rate of success would be one sale for every ten original prospects. It is a rule of thumb and maybe not too far off. But every situation is different.

Here's the thing. You have to start with large numbers on the front-end of the sales process to have smaller numbers for success at the back-end. To illustrate the point, I've selected the baseball metaphor. You can't score more runs than you have base runners cross each of the bases. Getting base runners from point to point along the base paths becomes the figurative sales process.

Getting to First Base: When you start out selling, it is the same as entering the batter's box. Unlike in baseball, getting to First Base in sales is easy. The process is to identify potential customers – specifically. This doesn't mean that the customer is generically in the tire business. It means that the potential customer is Ed's Tires on Center Street, and the owner/manager is Ed Talbot. In other words, you need to have all the information collected that you would need to contact Mr. Talbot. You are sitting on First Base when you have a complete database entry completed for the potential customer. Getting to First Base is so easy that it can even be accomplished by a person who isn't actually in sales, but just doing research. There is a 100% probability of getting to First Base.

Getting to Second Base: Armed with the data you've collected on a potential customer, the next step in the process is to make the initial call to them. These are often termed "cold calls." In reality, they don't have to be "cold" at all. The purpose of the first contact is to get an appointment to talk about the prospect's business and with an introduction to your business (but not an offer). You aren't directly selling the product yet when you are trying to advance to Second Base. You are just trying to get the appointment and some quality time with the prospect. You are sitting on Second Base once the appointment is confirmed. There should be a high conversion rate from First Base to Second Base. Just like in baseball, now you are in "scoring position."

Getting to Third Base: This is where the process becomes a little more challenging.   The base path between Second and Third Base is designated for developing a relationship with the customer. It includes introducing the product to the customer. But, and this is very important, it also includes listening hard and learning what the customer's needs really are. The goal is to be able to articulate customer needs in terms of your product offering. You are sitting on Third Base when the customer asks you to make a formal proposal or submission for your goods and services, with a price attached.

Some sales people like to dance off second base forever. With client dinners and complimentary tickets to events they think they are developing a relationship. The test is if and when the customer opens the door for a proposal. Failing that, you are probably in a figurative "run down," and it is just a matter of time before you are called out. Yet, with skill and experience, getting to Third Base can be a very high percentage play.

Getting Home and Scoring: Once the proposal is asked for, you are rounding Third Base.   Getting home depends on many variables, some beyond the control of the salesperson. Even with the best proposal possible there might be deficiencies in quality, fit, features, pricing, etc., which can render the proposal unacceptable – especially if this is a highly- competitive situation. The negotiating skills and closing skills of the salesperson go a long way toward increasing the probability of scoring. Often the entire organization, including senior management, needs to be engaged in the closing process.

After you Score (or are thrown out at the plate): The beauty of this sales metaphor is that it highlights a fundamental truth about the sales process – one that is important to embrace. The process continues after the initial decision is made, independent of the outcome. You are immediately back on Second Base, in scoring position. You no longer have to start in the batter's box to get to Second Base because all of that work has been accomplished. You can't imagine how many sales people are discouraged and fail to understand this important point. The game never ends. You should be back on the base paths trying to score again.

There are lots of innings and opportunities to score in the game of baseball. The same holds true for the sales game. Play ball!

42

GOOD SALES PEOPLE
ALWAYS SELL SOMEBODY

It didn't take me long after I left business school to be confronted with the importance of the sales department to the health and vitality of any organization. In academic circles the sales function is all but ignored. It's as if selling is a rote action performed by underlings, something similar to the "mow and blow" guys that do landscaping. I've consistently found that within most organizations the stature of "sales" isn't much further advanced. A sales department is a necessary evil, which would be promptly dispensed with if it were possible to have continuing and growing revenue from some invisible source. However, in my experience, *the sales department is the most indispensable part of the team.* As an early mentor of mine, Bud Fossler, once said: "If you can't sell it, you can't make it." Translation: without sales you can't make the product and you can't "make it" to survive.

What I have found is that the extraordinarily successful organizations overcome their prejudice and support a high-quality, well-drilled and professional sales organization. In fact, some companies actually have a reputation based on the selectivity and training they impose on their sales executives. *The most important point I can possibly make is to take the sales function seriously if you intend to be successful.* Further, there is nothing second-rate about a career in sales and sales management. I, for one, view it as a heroic calling.

With that as prelude, I would make the additional observation that not everyone can be successful at sales. I like to say that there is a "sales gene." This simply means that some people are cut out to be good at it and others aren't. I've found that it has absolutely nothing to do with intelligence (a fact that confounds really smart people). The success factor can be boiled down into one statement. Sales people love making sales calls. They would rather make sales call than do any other function. This is the defining element.

This is not to say that good sales people always work smart or efficiently. They don't. In fact it is almost a character deficiency that the very best sales people are the worst at managing their time or at preparing for their own sales calls. This is where the important role of sales manager comes into the picture. Sales people are like actors. The sales manager's role is to tell each of them where to stand and what to say. It is really just that simple. When complexity is added to this simple formula the results get worse – not better.

Excellence in sales management is much trickier than it looks. This is where to spend your time, money and training if you are trying to increase sales (with essentially the same product line). Investments in good sales management are likely to provide highly-leveraged returns on investment.

One of the best sales managers I ever worked with, Tim McNerney in Cincinnati, used to say something that I believe is absolutely true: "Good sales people always sell somebody." His rejoinder to this was: "It will either be the prospect, or it will be the sales manager." He was referring to the tendency of a sales person to come back to the manager to plead for a better offer, or a lower price, or some kind of incentive to convince the client to tip. He viewed his job as making it easier for the account executive to sell the prospect and harder for the sales person to sell him as the manager. He was creative when that was called for – writing good scripts for his actors. He was tough when that was called for. And, most of his sales staff knew that Tim could make the sale himself if they couldn't. He made me look like a hero for a number of consecutive sales periods. And, he left me with a piece of valuable insight – which I now share with you.

43

Ask for the order

How simple and straightforward is this advice? I'm almost embarrassed to include it in the book. Yet, this is a piece of advice that is constantly ignored, or at least subject to a syndrome of prolonged procrastination by managers and executives.

Where does this advice apply? Of course, it applies to selling situations. A person could never make a good living in sales if he or she weren't capable of asking for the order. This is the equivalent of the "never up, never in" adage in golf (when putting you must tap the ball as far as the hole if it is ever going to go in). In sales, there is a tendency to be so afraid of a negative answer that the order is never specifically asked for. How reasonable is this?

If you are going to get an order, you want to know sooner. If you are under consideration, but need to adjust your offer, you want to know that sooner. Even if you aren't going to get the order, you also want to know that sooner. You definitely don't want to keep wasting time on an order you'll never get. And you also want to start working on the next piece of business as soon as possible (back on Second Base). It is completely irrational to not want to know where you stand with a sales pitch – especially based on the fear of bad news.

The adage also applies to "internal" business interactions that occur in the workplace that aren't traditionally considered to be sales situations – when in fact they really are.

Where healthy businesses succeed is when decision makers and contributors share information. One person makes a decision but the others are expected to supply valuable input. *Both of these roles provide many opportunities for the people involved to sell each other.* Isn't that what really happens when you are trying to convince someone of a point of view or a course of action? Asking for the order is part of this sales process.

So, the question really is *when to ask for the order,* not if you should ask for the order. The "when" can be a tricky game depending on the individuals involved. You must be as prepared as possible to present your views convincingly - to sell your position. If you are being given the opportunity to provide advice, your contribution will depend on the consistency and the quality of advice you provide over time. If you are asking for advice you should be well-prepared in advance to evaluate the advice being given. Either way, preparation comes first.

The "how" of making the sales pitch depends on the nature of the invitation. You are either the inviter or the invited party. In both cases, be clear and crisp in defining the background, nature and scope of expected input in terms of the invitation. Put your advice in writing when possible. Even if the invitation doesn't require a written response, the process of writing something down is a good exercise to test whether your sales pitch is on target.

People trained at organizations like Procter & Gamble will recognize the exercise of creating the infamous "one page recommendation." This is a memo that proposes an action with complete background, metrics and next steps – all on a single page. I can remember my wife in her first year at P&G struggling with these documents for hours at home, honing her recommendations for submission to her boss (who was equally concerned that his or her name would be attached to the recommendation up the line). This was before computers and word processing. So, the documents became exercises in typing and multiple layers of correction fluid. Her boss felt compelled, as a teaching exercise, to send multiple iterations of her recommendations back to her with substantial red ink – lines, arrows and question marks – all over the document. It was initially disheartening to a new recruit. The purpose, of course, was to focus - really focus - on the sales pitch that was being made with all proper respect for the background and benefits for the business. Everyone in the organization was expecting to see information of this nature communicated efficiently in a standard format. Training of this nature lasts a lifetime.

Let's go back to the beginning. It is very important to ask for the order. This advances the cause and creates the creative velocity that high-performance businesses require. Knowing your role in the communications process is important for clarity. And, being succinct and direct is a necessary approach to advancing a cause. It all gets down to asking for the order.

THE "RULE OF THREE"

I will let you know this up front. I'm inventing my own rule and providing the justification. Whether or not you believe the rule has any merit for you is a personal decision. But if you read further, it might just make sense.

In the course of reading lots of articles in the business press and scouring reams of research data about media usage in all market sizes there is one recurring theme – if you look for it. The human brain is self-editing and also self-regulating. Because it has to work hard and rarely takes a rest, the brain seems to processes information in packets (much like the computer does). It is amazing to me how those packets tend to be in groupings of three. Maybe this is just my brain, and your brain works differently – in fours or fives perhaps. But upon reflection, I think you'll agree my novice neurological observation has merit.

In the world of consumer behavior there have been studies that demonstrate that too many choices actually confuse a potential buyer. Buyers tend to triage multiple choices down to a couple (for me this number is three), before they do detailed analysis leading to a final decision. In the old days, Sears had three grades of products – good, better and best.

In the broadcast media, audience surveys are constantly being conducted about the power of names and personalities in a market (radio or television). Study after study reveals the same pattern. With un-aided recall (no prompts or anyone helping) most people can only name 3-4 local personalities. More surprising is that they can't do much better with national TV personalities. Remember, these are the names and faces they see or hear multiple times every single day. Obviously, being one of the top 3-4 unaided recall names in the media is money in the bank. It is so important that people are inserted into jobs they have never done before to take advantage of this recall. For example: Katie Couric had strong name recognition but never did news anchoring before being selected by CBS News. As another example, until the advent of cable television there were only three major television networks. Now, perhaps many people can name a fourth. But, few can name a fifth or a sixth.

The point is that if the brain processes limited fields of information at any given time. A smart business person should know this and use it to maximum advantage. Why create long sentences with lots of phrases separated by commas when you can make shorter sentences, each with three simple thoughts? You can always add more sentences. Give the brain a rest. Why have PowerPoint presentations with a laundry list of bullet points? Create more slides, limiting each to 3-4 major points. When you put together goals, strategies and plans in a business document, limit them to three or four. Whether I'm right or wrong about the brain, instinctively I'll tell you that the process of focusing for brevity is always worth the effort.

When you expect someone to make a decision, try offering three choices – versus two, or four, or more. I think that I'm being manipulated in the marketplace when I have only two choices. Having more than three just makes my brain have to do extra work getting down to the best three (requiring two steps) – where I can confidently make a final selection.

I'm afraid my brain lives in a "small, medium or large" world. I'm just guessing that I'm not alone.

WHY IS THE GORILLA
ON THE ROOF?

This chapter is all about having a specific purpose behind doing advertising and promotions. It can be applied to many other areas of business practice. I owe this story to my friend Larry Anderson, the ultimate "radio guy" whom I first met at Taft Broadcasting. He later worked for me as the general manager of radio and concert properties in Wheeling, WV. Here is how he told the story:

There was a radio station manager in a medium-sized town that was very keen on having his stations be recognized in the home market. He constantly tried to use his creative skills to bring attention to his station. One day, he purchased a gorilla costume and came up with a plan to draw attention. On a busy Friday afternoon he dressed one of his interns up in the suit. Then he had the gorilla wave and dance at the edge of the roof, on the top of a multi-story building in the middle of town.

Sure enough. People started to notice the gorilla dancing at the roof's edge. In fact, so many people noticed the gorilla that a small crowd assembled on the sidewalk under the building. The people were intrigued by the gorilla dancing on the roof. The general manager looked out of his office window on the top floor of the building and was very pleased with himself as he saw the assembled crowd below.

One of the station's account executives was returning from outside appointments and had to walk through the assembled crowd on his way back to the station. Upon returning he was met by the station manager who excitedly asked him: "What are all the people saying?" The sales person answered: "They are all asking: Why is the gorilla on the roof?"

Of course, the moral of the story is that there wasn't a defined marketing or promotional value for all the time and effort expended. Sure, the stunt provided a collection of interested consumers with clear share of mind advantage. But what was the payoff? The gorilla never was tied back to the radio station or to the programs that they broadcast. The audience didn't know what to think. What was the value of doing this when the planning and strategy were so weak?

It would be easy to characterize this as a ridiculous story - one with no practical application. I beg to differ. If you just look around a little, you can easily spot the gorilla mistake being made, sometimes by supposedly sophisticated marketing organizations and agencies. It is so common that my wife and I watch television and ask ourselves if we can even remember the product name after we've seen a commercial the second time. The commercial may be memorable, but the product may not be. Or, how about the new restaurant in our home town that did a large newspaper advertisement to herald their grand opening? They even posted part of their menu in the ad. The only problem was that they failed to insert either the address or the telephone number of the new business.

As a simple business test, I find myself asking "Why is the gorilla on the roof?" when it comes to media and promotional spending. As a manager, you will be well-served by asking the same question.

SECTION VII
EXECUTION WISE

46

THERE IS ONLY ONE BALL

The most important reason that every young person should play a team sport of some kind is to understand that there is only one ball. Yes, exercise is a good and healthy reason for kids to be involved with youth athletics. But a child doesn't have to be part of a team for that. But every child needs to learn the lessons of playing on a team with one ball as a life skill. It is alarming the number of adults that either didn't learn the lessons of teamwork, or fail to employ them.

Very few activities in the real world are solo activities. There are none in business. Give me an example and I'll be able to prove to you that they really aren't done without the help of others somewhere along the way. Surgeons (a profession that is notoriously personality centric) need an entire medical team to be successful. Writers can sit alone and pen the greatest literature, but it goes nowhere without a team of experts to prepare a manuscript for publication. A composer can put the music and the lyrics on paper, but distribution to the world is dependent on musicians, performers and channels of distribution. The truth is that almost everything in life is a team game. In business, because transactions between two parties are present by definition, everything is a team game.

From years of coaching youth sports, and now from years of coaching executives, I will make the bold assertion that the most important thing for a leader, a follower or anyone on a team to understand is that there is only one ball.

A good team player can't hog the ball. It's not about personal glory.

A good team player can't play the game as if everybody has their own ball. This dilutes the concentrated effort that is required for success. And all success in business is ultimately team success, or should be.

A good team player can't ignore the ball, and slide into some passive-aggressive funk as a self-styled act of protest. If you don't like the game, or you don't like the team, or you don't like the coach of the team you must have the integrity to walk off the field. Maybe your game is slightly different. Baseball, basketball and soccer are very different sports. But, they all have a single ball. If you change jobs don't expect that there won't be a ball in play at your next assignment. There is always a ball.

The ball is the overall collective effort of the business or organization, always focused on achieving the goal. Sometimes it is parsed into parts with the guidance that a sub-goal is the focus of a smaller group. But, there is always a team, and they should always know what their ball is, and where it is relative to the goal. From that starting point, keeping the ball in play and moving toward the goal is central to business success. The very same thing applies to youth sports.

Get your children active in a team sport. Learn to play effectively on the team at work. *And, keep your eye on the ball.*

47

Don't buy a lottery ticket

Lotteries seem to be everywhere, as states vie to close budget shortfalls by inserting themselves into the business of legalized gambling. I rarely buy lottery tickets. On the occasions when I do it is because the payoff is gargantuan. So, I figure "what the heck." I'll spend a few bucks which I'll never miss on the outside chance to have a big payday. I view this as justifiable behavior even though I know that the chances of winning are slight (one in something like 1.4 billion). I also know that it is irrational behavior. It would be better if I saved the money or gave it to my church on Sunday for some positive social use. But every once in a while I can't help myself.

Most executives I know approach the whole lottery phenomena about the same way as I do. I can't remember ever being in the presence of a co-worker or one of my clients and making a special effort to go buy lottery tickets. Intelligent people all know the math and that the odds of winning are infinitesimal. In one of the ironies of life, it seems that the citizens buying lottery tickets are the least able to afford the purchase and would be better served by spending their money on some direct benefit to themselves – like food, shelter or transportation. Enough social commentary. The lure of the big payday (that can wash away all one's troubles) combined with the collective ignorance of the buying public are the two elements of the formula that makes sanctioned lotteries work in society.

What has any of this to do with business practice? Just this – I've been quite amazed to observe in my business life that well-trained executives will actually invest their money (or that of their company) into projects or activities that have very low probabilities of success. Maybe the chances of success are not one in a million. But certainly there can be an equation drawn that could put the chances of success at one in a thousand, or not better than one in a hundred. While the chances of a business success might be better as compared to lottery tickets, the cost of playing the game is also usually higher than "walking around money." In the end, what is really the fundamental difference between playing a lottery at work with company money and buying a ticket at a convenience store? I've thought about this a lot and I don't have an answer.

Explanations abound. Not answers. On one level, sometimes projects and initiatives are entered into with the promise of a modest investment yielding a large return. This is a rational business bet to make on its face. But what happens when things change? The amount needed to achieve the result keeps getting larger, and/or the potential return on the investment starts to shrink over time. Part way into the game the rules change. Now the math around this equation looks more and more like a lottery ticket. How many projects have you been involved that follow this pattern? The truth is, too many, or just about all of them.

Then there is the notion that a project may actually have two profiles. One is a spent and worthless lottery ticket to the company. The other has the profile of a winning ticket with annuitized payments to the individuals managing or working the project. What do I mean by this? Simply, many low yield projects are kept alive, often with false hope, by the very people who stand to benefit by the project being kept alive. There is a little demon saying: "Sure, the project is a bust, but as long as I'm getting paid, it is a great idea." This is also a very common thinking that can easily convert a perfectly good business bet at the outset into an expensive and worthless lottery ticket in the end.

So, what does the executive do? Every project and every initiative needs to be evaluated on a frequent basis (more than once a year) to determine: 1) how much money the company must invest to get any positive return? And, 2) what are the chances that the return will make such a high-risk position actually be worth it? The amount of money already invested is somewhat irrelevant when this calculation is being made. The number of jobs lost and the fortunes of the executives working the project are absolutely irrelevant. If you don't believe this, you may be engaged in an activity that is the equivalent of buying a lottery ticket.

48

CUT YOUR LOSSES SOONER

I have had ample opportunities to work with top CEOs from a variety of industries, in the work setting, in my consulting practice and by conducting CEO Boot Camps. If there is one consistent mistake that business leaders would like to correct in themselves, this would be the one. They have failed to cut their losses sooner. And they admit it.

The first inkling of this usually embarrassing failing is when there is a group discussion about underperforming personnel. A workshop technique that is effective is to have a CEO ask other CEOs for advice. The first volunteer's situation is described, often involving a single problem employee who either seems to be disruptive to the organization or beyond reclamation. The other CEOs chime right in and deliver the punch. "I'd get rid of that person." The irony occurs as we move to the next CEO in the round-robin discussion. It is typical that a similar set of circumstances is forthcoming, along with the same advice from the collective group. But this time the second CEO is cognizant of fact that he didn't follow his own clear advice for CEO number one. Very quickly, everyone in the group goes to the confessional and admits that this is their largest shortcoming.

Individual personnel decisions are probably just the tip of the proverbial iceberg, if an executive has a proclivity to procrastinate over decisions. The larger issues of which projects and initiatives should be continued and funded, versus those that should be put into immediate termination, are the troublesome ones. These are the ones that can make or break a career and have devastating effects on a company.

Getting these decisions right starts with a determined attitude not to make this classic mistake. In other words, you must be committed to cutting out unproductive projects or programs that have run their course as contributors to the overall health of the organization. In many instances these projects or divisions can be sold, sometimes to existing employees. This provides the added benefit of raising some cash in the process of off-loading the poor performer.

Beyond the determination of the leader, there is a need for timely and reliable data from which to make informed decisions. If an executive is having difficulty obtaining the proper data from down the line, there is a very good chance that the project or division is an underperformer. Guess who really isn't motivated to provide the information? That would be anyone likely to suffer the consequences of an adverse decision. How many times do we have to observe this behavior in the real world to know that it is commonplace?

Data are an interesting culprit in many instances. Would it surprise you to learn that a survey (*Wall Street Journal,* March 15, 2006) shows that fewer than 20%

of college basketball teams that are behind at halftime actually make a comeback and win the game? Yet, the fans in the stands remain optimistic and cheer their team to win well into the second half. It is not so surprising that the same attitude is transferred to business behavior – where my guess is that the odds of success are equally as long. But we like to believe in the underdog. Moreover, executives like to believe that things will change for the better because it is easier – until it turns out to be much harder down the road.

An impediment to cutting losses is the trepidation that the executive in charge feels toward actually doing it the right way. So, the decision is clear, but the holdup is that the steps to accomplish the goal are unclear. Unhealthy organizations can wallow in this swamp of indecision. If the exorcism isn't accomplished with care and precision, the thought is that the company could suffer some losses in the process. So, executing the decision is delayed, often multiple times, and the company is then guaranteed to suffer even more losses against a strategic decision that has already been made.

In the final analysis, this is a lot like dating (something most of us haven't done in a while, yet we can still identify our scars from the process). If there is no sense in continuing a strategic relationship, move on. Time is a valuable resource to waste. When excess time delays cost extra money and create heartburn, it is even more difficult to justify.

So, cut your losses sooner. Your fellow CEOs are on the sidelines, cheering for you to do this. I've heard them loud and clear.

49

TAXI CABS HAVE A
GOOD BUSINESS MODEL

I know, this sounds like an unlikely title for a chapter about business strategy, but bear with me.

Consider the taxi driver in a large city like New York or Chicago. By law, if the taxis are empty they are supposed to stop when hailed, no matter the extenuating circumstances. They are, after all, licensed (under a fixed numerical cap) as part of the public transportation infrastructure, although I doubt that any would describe their role in such lofty terms as a service to society.

Have you ever noticed that a taxi driver will cut across multiple lanes, or do a U-turn in traffic, to get to the curb when a potential passenger has heaps of luggage and appears to be going to the airport? Why does this happen? The behavior is beyond excessive and well beyond what a cab driver would do for a supermodel teetering on high-heels, juggling shopping bags and waving madly. Personally, I'd rather have the supermodel as a passenger and it has nothing to do with stealing glances in the rear view mirror. More about that later.

It appears that taxi drivers covet trips to the airport. They even hang out in lines at hotels to increase their chances of grabbing these trips. Why? It gets them out of the congested stop-and-go city. They are able to drive faster and enjoy the sensation of getting somewhere. When they get to the airport, there is always the trip back (double the pay-off), even if they must sit in a queue behind other cabs waiting for a return trip. This isn't so bad either if there is a newspaper to read. It's even better with a cigarette or a cup of coffee. Yeah, cab drivers have it all figured out. This is why they will risk life and limb to snatch rides to the airport. If you ever want to test this theory just hold out a sign that says "Airport," especially if you don't have any luggage but you really need to get there in a hurry.

Notice that I said that the drivers have it figured out. This all changes when the drivers own their own cabs and they effectively become "business managers" (versus hourly employees) of their own enterprise. Then the tendency is to look for that supermodel, or the elderly person, or the impatient investment banker late for a meeting, or a person in a clown suit – in fact anybody that looks like they aren't going to the airport. What's the big difference? Why the change in attitude?

The answer is in the simple business concept of the "meter drop." Each time the cab picks up a new rider, the driver resets the meter, and immediately a large initial sum (currently $2.50 in New York) becomes due. Remember, the cab hasn't even left the curb, and now the owner of the cab is $2.50 to the good. The $.40 per unit (about $2.00 per mile) is fine, but this amount comes with wear and tear on the cab – variable operating expenses if you will. So, you do the math. Is it better to have one round trip to the airport, at 50 miles (with two meter drops) or that same 50 miles of travel (with 10 meter drops) taking the exact same amount of time?

The answer is obvious. Not surprisingly, enterprising drivers eventually figure out that they will make more money too. Multiple opportunities for tips are better than just a couple (more soft "meter drops") – therefore more money in their pocket. Isn't capitalism great?

This example points to the simple truth that "meter drops" – we call them "recurring revenue" in business – are very valuable propositions. Why wait for payouts, either large or small ones, which are in the distant future and perhaps unsure, when you can invest in, or own, a (figurative) taxi cab? Of course, you must always do the analysis and one size doesn't fit all. But, I've tried to remain conscious of this simple example when I've been in a position to analyze or invest in a business. Layer onto this thinking that the number of taxi cabs in large cities is usually fixed (there is actually a market for buying and selling medallions in New York and they sell for hundreds of thousands), and you have another attractive business concept – barriers to entry. For years the broadcasting business has flourished under the same approximate business model as the taxi cab.

So, when you are out "driving your business around town," start picking up those supermodels. Even if they don't tip much, you'll still make more money. And you might get a good story to tell as a bonus.

50

INCREMENTAL IMPROVEMENTS YIELD THE HIGHEST FINANCIAL RETURNS

There are two fundamental premises to embrace in order to understand fully this piece of advice:

1) It is almost always harder to start a business or enterprise from scratch than it is to build onto something that has already gone through some of the initial growth pains. This relates to the generally accepted business premise that it is easier, cheaper and faster to "buy," rather than to "build."

2) It is much easier to grow something in small increments than to grow it in large increments. Said another way, it is easier to grow a business by 10% (top line) in a year, than it is to grow it by 50%.

In football terms, this chapter is making the case for achieving scores through progressions of first downs, as opposed to relying exclusively on the "Hail Mary" pass. There are three scenarios.

Company not making any money.

This is the classic case where expenses are higher than gross revenue. It might not be wise, or even possible, to reduce expenses further. To get to profitability the revenue needs to improve. The case where there is zero revenue is the toughest one. This is the accounting equivalent of starting from scratch. But if there are any prospects for revenue, view the challenge as incrementally improving the revenue to close the gap. Of course, this only works with a series of incremental sale or price improvements. The failure of a business to be able to make steady incremental improvements to the top line is tantamount to diagnosing a death sentence. In Chapter 26 we talked about there being "no silver bullets," so escape from failure is effectively denied in the absence of incremental improvements. It is hard for executives to accept that.

Company just breaking even.

In many ways this is the most interesting case. The assumption is that revenues are just covering expenses. Tinkering with expenses might help the bottom line and this is the classic approach taken by private equity firms. Their view is that expenses that are cut immediately mean that profits drop to the bottom line immediately. Then there is a chance of selling out of the business with a leveraged gain. Never mind that cutting expenses might not be wise. There is as much leverage into bottom-line results by just expanding the revenue base. Many businesses are structured so that fixed costs don't go up with increased sales, and the margins on variable costs are quite attractive. So, a small increase in revenues might yield a large percentage change in profits because most of the new revenue drops like a stone to the bottom line. Again, buy-out guys live to find these situations. They are almost giddy when they can increase sales incrementally while also cutting expenses.

Company making money.

Consultants like me are almost never called into these situations. But we should be. This is one of the most fertile valleys in business. The private equity players crave finding companies doing well which are managed poorly. They know the power of streamlining management while at the same time adding horsepower to the sales process. It is the classic win-win. Companies in the position of doing well really owe it to themselves to have comprehensive, periodic check-ups from the outside. Without one, they may never know if they are maxing-out their business. There is such tremendous bottom line power by doing simple things to improve the existing business that they should welcome the process. Sadly, few do. From my experience, the sweet-spot in consulting is when a company which has been doing well suddenly finds itself in trouble – headed for just breaking even, or even maybe losing a little money. That is when panic emerges. But the medicine is the same as in all the other cases. There must be incremental improvements in the business to reverse the trend. Small changes have large effects.

The real irony is when a company does reverse the trend, and then decides that it no longer needs the periodic evaluations that an outsider can provide. This happens more often than not. As a good friend of mine says, "stupid is forever." That will be a chapter in my next book!

51

YOU CAN'T MANAGE
WHAT YOU CAN'T MEASURE

I believe this is one of Peter Drucker's adages. If it isn't, then it should have been because it is typical of his style: direct and to the point.

As a manager, there is no chance for success if you don't know where you've been, where you are, and where you are going. It really is pretty simple and straightforward. *You are only able to determine the relative position of your situation with data.* In business, data are usually converted into numbers, or numerical benchmarks. So, numbers are unavoidable in the management of any business or enterprise of consequence.

So, why do so many people in management seem to be always trying to avoid or ignore the numbers? This is a good question, and one that has many answers.

1) Some individuals may be brilliant (like a musician or an artist), but they fundamentally don't have an aptitude for numbers. It doesn't make these individuals inferior or socially crippled. It is a plain fact of life. As a consequence, non-numerate people shouldn't be put into positions of management. They won't succeed, because

they can't. It is a manager's job to avoid placing people in no-win situations. This is about the biggest no-win imaginable.

2) Some individuals understand data and numbers, but they don't want to invest the effort it takes to master them. These people are fundamentally lazy. They don't have a numbers problem, but they do have an attitude problem. There is only one cure, a change in attitude. There is only one conclusion for a manager that has an employee like this in a management position who won't change – termination. Bad attitudes in reporting data should never be tolerated for long in organizations with reporting requirements.

3) Then there are those that actually understand the numbers, but are afraid to acknowledge the picture they paint and the consequences of acting upon the data. This is another kind of management challenge, because the root can either be bad attitude (see above) or fear. The two tell-tales to fear are that the manager becomes crippled (with slow or no actions) or delusional (with swift, but irrational actions). Neither is to be preferred. Both are problematic.

4) Then there are those that actually understand the numbers and ignore them – not out of fear or delusion – but because they believe that they possess superhuman powers. They aren't confined to the laws of mathematics when it comes to their personal success. To a certain extent, all good sales people fall into this category. The jump from successful sales person to sales manager is often a long one, for just this very reason. There are delusional elements to this. But the dominant attitude is that there is no possibility for retreat or defeat. It just isn't in the vocabulary.

5) Then there are people that understand numbers,

but they need help in interpreting the numbers and converting them into strategies and tactics. They are worth the time and effort to train. The test of this is their willingness to learn and become more decisive.

The best of all worlds is to have managers that know the numbers, what they mean and what they indicate as benchmarks for future action. This puts us squarely back at the beginning of this chapter.

You can't manage what you can't measure.

52

IT IS BETTER TO INSPECT RESULTS
THAN TO EXPECT RESULTS

I first heard my first variation of this common adage from a retired Procter & Gamble executive turned consultant, Dick McKinney. This was many years ago, and it made a big impression. Not only because of the words, but because of the source – a person I respected from a company I respected. The abbreviated version of the same adage is: "Inspect what you expect."

The guidance is simple. People respond with better behavior if they believe that the boss is watching. It works for many reasons, on multiple levels. It works because a person may be afraid of losing their job if performance isn't up to standard. The more you check performance the clearer that message becomes. It works because some people work hard for recognition and more performance checks mean more opportunities for applause. It works because employees are more inclined to believe that you care about the overall business (and ultimately their own job security) if you demonstrate this with regular performance reviews. Getting rid of "bad apples" in the workforce reinforces the point.

But, the adage also takes a swipe at some prevalent and fuzzy thinking in the executive ranks of many companies and organizations. The thinking is that if the boss declares something the organization will automatically fall in line to achieve the specified objectives, goals and tactical results. I hate to burst this bubble, but it ain't so. The expectations of a leader have very little to do with creating incentives for an individual, or a collection of individuals, to perform in a certain manner. Yes, there is the element of charisma. But long-term charisma alone won't get the job done.

When expectations are reinforced with an element of fear, this can create a positive incentive to adjust behavior. For example, society expects that "no parking" signs will be obeyed and the penalty for not doing so reinforces the expectation. There is inherent fear built into inspections which shouldn't be destructive – the fear of not delivering on a promise made to the organization can be positive.

But the business of getting performance out of individuals and organizations is complicated. If you care about your business and the people contributing to your business, that's a good start. If you have a clear goal and a workable plan, people will tend to have trust in you as a leader. And, if you inspect their work, they will know that you are serious about results. They will know that *"you mean business."*

53

DRAW FAST
AND SHOOT STRAIGHT

In the course of doing on-boarding for new senior executives, and in executive coaching, one situation reappears consistently which creates a high degree of uncertainty and anxiety. It is how to handle a highly-charged question from a superior.

First off, we all have bosses. So, what I'm about to describe is a business problem for everyone. Secondly, not being prepared for this situation can have disastrous consequences for you and your career.

Here's the scene. Your boss sets up a private meeting with you. He or she looks you in the eye and asks: "Tell me what you really think about such and such, or so and so." What do you do next? This is something that is bound to happen, so it wouldn't be a waste of time to do some advance preparation. Rehearsing answers to possible questions ahead of time makes sense. You're not likely to get any advance warning as to when a question will be popped.

My first advice to managers that ask me how to handle this ambush is to be very careful about evaluating the situation. Is this an insecure person who asks these kinds of questions of everyone, trying to keep them off balance? Is this a devious person, trying to set you up in an untenable position where all you have is lose-lose possibilities? Or, is this a person who has come to trust you, and really is looking for advice to use in a serious matter – where they must make an important decision soon? Knowing the personality, character and motives of the questioner will be crucial for you to handle the question well. Being prepared with the "what if" answer, in case you are ambushed, will also provide you with some comfort and clarity as to the answer. By the way, questions like this are almost always asked. If you don't get a question like this, be worried. It means that you haven't earned the right to contribute or criticize within your organization.

With the insecure person, you might want to frame the answer in a way that reflects back at them. The answer should bolster their confidence – period. This isn't someone to tell the whole truth to. If you have bad news, leak it generally with a shock-absorber, so it doesn't have an equal and opposite reaction that bumps you. In many ways, this is the easiest to handle because you don't have to lie. Lying is a bad personal strategy. But, you don't have to tell the whole truth either. Never make it personal.

The devious boss is a waste of corporate time and talent. But we've all run into people that went to the J.R. Ewing School of Management (for those unacquainted with reference, J.R. Ewing was a nasty character from the 1980's hit TV series *Dallas*). There is no escaping damage when someone like this asks you a pointed question. All you can do is deflect the question cleverly and hope the damage is minimal. Absolutely, don't tell the whole truth because you'll be writing your own pink slip. Just hope that the organization eventually recognizes the person for what he or she is and makes an internal adjustment. If this is a family-owned business and a family member confronts you – duck. Then think about getting a new job, on your terms, over whatever time it takes. This is organizational cancer and it devours everything in its path until the organism is dead. There is no business medicine to stop it.

Now, for the really serious advice. Along the way, you'll work for very hard-working, sincere and receptive bosses. When they ask you this question they are entrusting you with their vulnerability and they will only have respect for you if you respond with complete and thoughtful honesty. This is what they want, and this is what they expect you to provide. Here, there is only one long-term strategy that will work if you want to continue a relationship with this person over time. You must draw fast (enough) and shoot straight.

I learned this advice from one of my most able bosses, Carl Wagner, the radio group head at Taft Broadcasting. Like so many successful executives, he came from modest, but rock-solid family roots and was a person that had worked hard for his success – often taking on the most difficult tasks. I had enormous respect for Carl as a mentor and boss, and I still do as a trusted friend (he has been happily retired for many years). But, there came the fateful day when he asked me the first time (of many) for my honest opinion on a serious business matter. Being young and insecure myself, I started to do the "rope-a-dope." Carl stopped me mid-sentence and gave me this advice. He said: "Mark, you and I are a lot alike. Nobody ever gave us anything. I've learned over time that there is only one way to respond to a question like the one I'm asking you. *Draw fast, and shoot straight.*" It was valuable advice that I have never forgotten.

I must confess that I've adjusted my thinking in a small way just recently. I was reading about Wyatt Earp, the legendary lawman and iconic figure from America's folk history. Gunfights at high noon, with two adversaries drawing pistols on Main Street are more myth than reality. But shoot-outs were very real. Earp's advice was to draw slowly and shoot to kill. Similarly, in business the speed of your response should be measured. But the answer to the question must be dead-on. I don't believe Carl will mind being modified by the experience of Wyatt Earp.

54

BORBELY'S LAW:
POLITICS WILL PREVAIL

Borbely's Law is pretty straightforward, and applies universally to all organizations. *When all is said and done, politics will prevail.*

My friend Bill Borbely is a successful entrepreneur. When I casually mentioned to him that I was writing a book about real-world lessons in business, he proffered his own contribution to the cause. He mentioned that he has always wanted to write a book about his "Law." I'll borrow it for something a little shorter.

Rather than debate whether Borbely's Law is true or false, or whether it is good or bad, let's move instead to the practical application of politics, which we all can agree is a fundamental force in decision-making for all organizations – business or other. The internal and external politics surrounding all decisions are as pervasive as gravity. Because politics always seems to be there, we tend to pre-assume them, even to the point of forgetting their influence on our behavior. But politics never go away.

So, how do we parse this one out as managers and executives? When we are in control, it is probably a good idea to diminish the pressures of internal politics on situations and decisions. The reason for this is instinctively simple – it is harder to do the right thing(s) when there is an overhang about how decisions will play elsewhere within the organization. It is like carrying extra weight around in your backpack. It is tough enough to do the right things, or what you and your team believe are the right things, without the burden of always looking over your shoulders. This approach works well within encapsulated groups and teams that are small and nimble. If the executive is able to lift the weight of politics off the team the results will always be better.

But, as a practical matter, politics are virtually unavoidable in larger organizations. These would include church hierarchies, academic institutions and non-profit charitable organizations every bit as much as business enterprises. This is because with numbers come multiple personal agendas. It is really that simple. An undeniable fact of human nature is that individually we have a strong inclination to want things done our own way. Putting individuals into group settings is often a volatile mix, and politics emerge as part of the solution, while at the same time becoming part of the problem.

Some individuals are able to overcome the prejudices of their own views and become great team players and leaders. It is no surprise that businesses have gravitated to hiring people with either military or sports backgrounds. The advantage to these people within a group is that they have some training and practical success in side-stepping some of the political nonsense. If they don't, they have experience in "playing the political game" at the very least.

We grudgingly acknowledge that politics is the necessary grease to lubricate an organization so that gears can generate actions. But, we also know that political stress can be the weight around an organization that will slow it down from achieving full potential. Where is the balance? This has to be determined case by case, organization by organization, business by business. If you are the person in charge you have the possibility of influencing the organization away from needless layering of politics and potentially destructive behavior. But, if you are stuck inside an organization, the political challenges are real, immediate and consequential. It is always good to be perceived as a team player, putting group success ahead of personal success. Sacrificing a personal agenda can be an effective technique to deliver a "knockout punch" at the appropriate moment to overcome political insanity. The worst behavior of all is becoming passively aggressive. If you see this happening to your own attitude, it is probably time for a personal change.

Borbley's Law is something to ponder in every situation. I hope Bill actually writes the book on how to deal with political force fields, which like gravity are ever-present. I'd buy the first copy.

55

SUCCESS ALWAYS
DEPENDS ON SURVIVAL

Over the years I've had many opportunities to evaluate or work with start-up and early-stage businesses – scores of them. While there are countless reasons for new businesses to fail, one of the recurring themes with entrepreneurs is that they tend not to give themselves enough figurative "runway" to succeed. They underestimate the time it will take to build the business and get ahead of themselves in planning for the time when they will be wildly successful. But success depends on survival. There is usually scant little in most business plans about surviving a string of disappointments and reversals. It is one reason why so many new businesses fail. So let's dissect the causes of this epidemic of carelessness.

First, businesses are often started by dreamers (without the benefit of the other two personalities needed for success – businessman and the son-of-a-bitch). Dreamers are in love with their creations. This is to be expected and has benefits. But, because they are dreamers, they envision a world where their ideas have already achieved success. Sometimes they are already formulating the next generation of the idea or working on a completely new idea. Dreamers tend not to be realistic. They have characteristics similar to hummingbirds, which are always in motion and they dart from flower to flower. So, the mundane exercise of putting together the plan for success, and insuring enough time for success, are among the last things that dreamers are concerned with. In doing this, they expose their business to possible failure.

Some entrepreneurs assemble a thorough business plan. Often, there is a team of people starting a business and one is assigned to tackle this project (some of my consulting has been along these lines). With certainty, any source of funding will be concerned with long-term viability of the plan. The gap often occurs when the new business is being funded by the entrepreneur(s) directly, or some group cobbled together from friends and family. Two things can predictably happen: 1) the plan is informal, and 2) the amount of start-up capital is significantly less than is needed (if you haven't tried, it is hard to get friends and family to commit large sums of their hard-earned money). The lack of a good plan can be fatal. But the lack of sufficient capital almost always is. So, perfectly viable business ideas may be destined to fail because they can't meet the survival hurdle.

Sometimes, there are good written plans and there is enough capital to survive. But even that may not be enough. I've found that there is tendency for things to take twice as long as initially thought and to cost twice as much. One mistake is to ignore contingencies in the planning or the funding process. The more prevalent mistake is to ignore the signs that things are going slower than planned and then not adjust to a survival plan. This implies spending less on development, perhaps reducing the work force and limiting marketing dollars to only those programs with direct results.

The enthusiastic entrepreneur has a difficult time doing any of these things. So, they try to save the business by frantically looking for more money. Fundraising takes time. When you are under stress, it takes too much time. The cost of getting additional money under stress is very high and the entrepreneur can forfeit a large ownership stake just to compensate for the lack of a contingency plan or an unwillingness to slow down the process of development and growth. The combination of failing to make changes and failing to raise additional capital is by definition fatal. It might have been avoided.

You must survive to succeed. Plan for survival first. Plan for success after that. I tell all my clients that before they can become a successful big business they must become a successful small business. It is logical to say it, and I think they understand the principle. But putting the principal into practice is annoying. We depend on entrepreneurs to be our economic growth engine. The world loves dreamers. The success of the figurative "two guys in a garage" becomes legendary (eBay, Google, Microsoft, Apple, etc.) when they succeed.

But statistically most new businesses fail. And, they don't have to. All they have to do is survive.

SECTION VIII
PEOPLE WISE

56

THERE IS ONLY
ONE KIND OF MOTIVATION,
SELF-MOTIVATION

There are a couple of indelible recollections from my business school days. One is of the first day of class for one of the "core courses," as they were known then, Management 101. I don't recall the professor's name, but I do clearly remember how he opened the class. His message was: "Management is about making things happen and involves getting leaders and followers moving in the same direction. Therefore, it is easy to assume that management starts with motivation. My experience has been that there is only one kind of motivation, self-motivation. People do something either by habit or because it is in their own self-interest. What gets you or someone else to decide do something is incentives – not motivation. What the remainder of this course will be about is incentives."

I don't remember the remainder of the course. The textbook was expensive and the package of extra reading materials for the course was thick. I did pass. But, I've often marveled that this was among the best minutes of learning that I've ever experienced. The light went on for me. I've learned to appreciate this insight more and more as time goes by.

When you look around, it is startling how simple and clear my former professor really had it figured. It didn't make the study of management issues any less complicated. But it did frame one of the fundamental challenges that all executives face when attempting to get something done. It is good when a leader has a sense of direction, has a plan. Then it is essential that the leader communicate clearly the direction being taken and why. But for the followers to sign-on it is important to provide the pay-offs for making personal behavioral decisions that accomplish the mission. Make no mistake about this, the followers always frame their decision to sign-on and do something in this context: "What's in it for me if I do, and what happens if I don't." So, it comes down to self-motivation. That means using incentives, or in some cases, disincentives.

What incentives are in your portfolio when you attempt to get someone to self-motivate? I'd include all the usual suspects: greed, fear, pride, guilt, friendship, trust, pleasure and pain. It is a long list. The art of management is actually to provide the right "incentive formula" to get a team or an individual moving in the desired direction. It isn't as if motivation were an external force. It is taking advantage of the fundamental nature of self-motivation.

You don't need to look too hard to find successful organizations and leaders that practice the incentive game. The military has its own unique formula to mold individuals into working units which has been proven to work. Even organized religions have their own recipes for success. The successful leaders aren't really motivators at all. They are more like chemists.

Allow me to insert a personal observation. The positive incentives (like greed and pleasure) work a lot better than the negative ones (fear, poverty, pain) over the long term. So, if you actually think that you'll need to maintain your leadership position by continually providing effective incentives, first consider the positive and enduring ones. Short term negative incentives do work. But leave a couple of these bullets in your gun only as back-up. Bad leaders, and many inexperienced new leaders, tend to resort to threats and punishments as the first tools in their tool box. If you are leaning much away from a balance of 95% "carrot" and 5% "stick," you probably have it wrong and need to recalibrate in a hurry.

57

THE TEXAS EMPLOYEE
INCENTIVE PLAN

Having been born and raised in New England, and then having spent most of my business life in the Midwest, I wasn't prepared for the cultural awakening I experienced when we relocated to Texas. At first skeptical, our family learned to embrace and relish the special pride and resourcefulness that is manifest in Texas. Living there is truly a "state of mind." On top of that, Texas people collectively are the nicest we have ever known.

An example of their straightforward attitude was found taped to the wall behind the cash register of a sporting goods store in a small Texas town (I forget which one, but somewhere near San Antonio). It simple stated: "Our Employee Incentive Plan – Work hard or you are fired."

I appreciate the simplicity. I like the sentiment. In a world were there is a tendency to make things more complicated than they are, or to wrap them with endless "psycho-babble," this simple statement was refreshing. Sometimes we need to be reminded of the essential facts.

What more can I say? This isn't the kind of hand-made sign you'd be likely to find in Massachusetts or California. As another sign I once saw stated: "Texas isn't for amateurs." Amen.

58

THEY DON'T CARE HOW MUCH
YOU KNOW, UNTIL THEY KNOW
HOW MUCH YOU CARE

Some adages are so powerful and clear that they hardly need to be expanded upon. This is one of those.

I first heard this in Nashville when a candidate I was interviewing for sales manager at a radio station provided this phrase as the underlying approach that she would follow if given the position. I'd never quite heard it put this way before, although managers (the good ones anyway) are inclined to be "people oriented," a catch phrase you commonly hear. To anticipate the reader's question, this candidate got the job. It wasn't because of her clever answer, but because she fit the three important criteria of competency, attitude and fit with the organization.

The essence of the wisdom here can be broken into two parts – both of which we discuss in other adages. First, there is only one kind of motivation – self motivation. So, people (remember, employees are people) only do the things well that they really want to do at all. Second, of the possible incentives that inspire self-motivation, trusting that a manager is concerned about an employee's well-being is at the top of list. People don't stay in working situations very long where they think the boss is mean, unfair and heartless, while they will tolerate technical incompetence for long stretches.

This observation actually highlights one weakness to an otherwise effective adage. It isn't uncommon to run into a manager of a project or a division who is completely ineffective, but beloved by the employees. This "caring condition" creates an absurd and convoluted kind of job security for incompetence. Executives, beware of this pothole. It is akin to tenure in private industry. Every reason in the book will be used to convince you not to make a change, when one clearly is called for based on performance.

For the good manager, wanting to get better, letting people know how much you care can be a powerful tool. Some executives do this instinctively and naturally. Others may have to fake it a bit. Either way, it always seems to work because the employees want to believe that it is true. Unfortunately, executives (and by association the cultures of companies) get painted in terms of wearing a "white hat" or a "black hat." Everyone is cheering for the "white hats" and wants to be part of that kind of group. Likewise, everyone despises the "black hats." It is all but impossible to change the perception of being a "black hat" once the scales have tipped.

The secret of the adage is that getting people to follow you isn't about the brilliance of the plan. It is about the trust you have earned. This is the reason that outside consultants can't be entrusted with executing a plan. They don't have any figurative "trust" on the balance sheet. It is also why the mistrusted executive can't fully execute the plan without substantial turnover in the lower ranks. It is easier to start over than to rebuild trust.

Caring about others is a lesson that we learn in elementary school, but fail to practice in business settings. Who really likes and trusts the smartest kid in the class, especially when that converts to becoming the teacher's pet? Children instinctively like and respect the lesser intellects who demonstrate the ability to be complimentary, who don't "hog the ball" in sports, and who don't talk down their classmates behind their backs. Once in a while, the smartest kid in the class actually does all the right things and builds trust among the peer group. Find that person as an adult and you have the power to achieve great things.

If you aren't that person today, find a way to become that person. A great place to start is to let people know how much you care.

59

JOHNNY BENCH WAS THE GREATEST CATCHER, BUT NOT A GOOD THIRD BASEMAN

To provide the proper context, I must inform the reader that for many years our family had the pleasure of living next door to Johnny Bench. He was a great neighbor in every possible regard. Don't get either my son or me into a discussion about who the greatest all-time catcher is. We know the answer and can recite the statistics. And, don't get my wife into a discussion about whether or not John was a great community influence and a role model off the field. She doesn't care all that much for baseball. But she is big on measuring character. Needless to say, we all have genuine affection for our friend and former neighbor.

At least one aspect of John's baseball career provides an interesting perspective into business practice. Late in his career with the Cincinnati Reds, management asked him to try playing third base. The purpose was to save his aging knees while keeping the all-time Reds home run leader in the daily line-up. On paper, the move made sense. In reality, it didn't fully achieve the intended results. In 107 games at third, Bench committed 19 errors and his batting average for the season dropped from .309 to .258. John was a natural as a catcher, but not at third base. He became frustrated by the inconsistency of his fielding and this probably affected his hitting. I don't know this for sure, but if you asked John what his most frustrating season was, I suspect it would be the one I've highlighted above – 1982, when he was only thirty-four.

Let's break it down. You start with arguably the greatest player ever to play a position – in the entire history of the game. Then management moves him ninety feet to third base and he turns into just another utility infielder. Everything else stays the same. The uniforms, the teammates, the opposing pitchers – essentially every other variable remains unchanged. The only difference is ninety feet (and perhaps those aging knees).

The story is instructive because in business there is always a tendency to move a star player from a position where their performance is outstanding to another assignment where the prospects are at best doubtful. When ultimately measured they don't achieve the desired result, creating a crisis for the organization. How different is this from the sports analogy that I'm suggesting above? One of the problems with personnel moves in business is that you can't reverse a mistake by simply changing the line-up card the next day. The moves are more permanent than with a sports team that plays frequently and re-groups every season.

Thinking about this story, the smart manager has three challenges. Every player must be evaluated against the position being played. First, some players don't even belong on the team (another issue altogether). Second, some players are in the wrong positions and need to be moved (up, down or sideways) into positions where they can become stars. Third, some players are in exactly the correct positions. If this is the case, and it is obvious, why hurt the player and the team by moving him or her to a place where they are likely to fail?

A delicate situation emerges when the player wants to be moved either for a change of venue or for a promotion, a move the manager is pretty sure won't result in a happy ending. Do you promote the person on the hope that success will "just happen" in spite of the odds going in? Or, do you not grant the promotion, knowing that by doing so you are creating disappointment for the person which may result in their leaving the team all together? This is a tough call. In some regards, it is the dreaded "no win."

Perhaps a good starting point is having a frank discussion with the employee concerned. Start with the story of Johnny Bench. The employee might appreciate having this perspective added to their own thinking on the matter. At the very least, they will understand that you are as concerned about their well-being as you are about the well-being of your team.

And just maybe, this will be another clutch hit brought to you by the greatest catcher ever. Just ask us.

60

WHERE TO PLAY BABE RUTH?

For many years my son and I have played a game together to pass the time while we've been taking cross-country automobile trips. It started when he was about ten and continues to this day, although now that he is twenty-eight and with the schedule of a surgical resident we have precious few opportunities to play. The game goes like this. We pick a sport and an era and then we try to assemble the "greatest team" of individual players by position. Along the way we have to justify to each other the reasons for including the player. The game gets very interesting when we pick the "all-time" greatest teams by position.

We've been playing this game for years, and we always get into a huge dilemma when it comes to baseball where the eras and the players are actually difficult to compare because the statistics aren't easy to compare due to changes in the game (for example, night baseball or the designated hitter – not to mention the recent steroid usage scandal). When we are done with the game we laugh at ourselves because we always seem to fall into the same trap. Where do we play Babe Ruth? As a right fielder he really wasn't much. In fact, some speculate that right field in old Yankee Stadium was specifically designed to suit the "Sultan of Swat," with a short fence for hitting home runs and a small area for the rotund Ruth to cover. There are many viable all-around candidates with better fielding skills to put into this position on the field – names like Hank Aaron and Roberto Clemente, both Hall of Famers. So, you see where this is going. Where do you play Babe Ruth? Many baseball experts argue that Ruth was the greatest baseball player of all time, with both statistical and cultural justification.

What does all this have to do with business? Just this. In many business situations I've encountered managers who are faced with a nearly parallel situation. It comes in two familiar variations.

First, there is oftentimes a person in the organization that is so good at everything that it becomes a dilemma as to where to put him or her in the organization for maximum benefit. This person might even be a threat to take the job of a manager if anyone higher in the organization knew how good he or she was. So, the natural inclination of the executive is to put this person into the slot that they need filled – often among the most difficult and least rewarding positions in the entire enterprise. Lo and behold, this person succeeds beyond everyone's wildest imagination and everyone is happy. Right? Well, not always. It turns out that the employee may figure out the game, know that they have gotten a rotten assignment and really not enjoy playing the position to which they were assigned (sometimes with the promise that it would only be temporary). I can't tell you how many times I see truly outstanding business players buried in the bowels of an organization. The bad manager lets this fester. The good manager is faced with a question: "Where do I play Babe Ruth (now)?"

The second flavor of the dilemma works differently. Everyone knows that there is an exceptionally gifted (one in a million) player on the team. And, everyone knows that this person will dominate the part of the organization they are assigned to, potentially exposing the other players as weak or ineffective as the "star" makes things happen. At the very least resentment will be created. So, while the outstanding player is respected throughout the organization, nobody really wants them on their team, unless they are in deep trouble and need a "messiah." Let's say, to add further complexity, that the star really doesn't have the "management gene" and must be put on the field in a day-to-day position. And, we could complicate this even more by mentioning that the star really believes he is a star and acts like one. He or she may in fact think that they should be the boss (as Babe Ruth did), thus positioning themselves as a disruptive force on the team.

Managing stars is very difficult. Managing super-stars is nearly impossible. So again, the good manager is faced with the question: "Where do I play Babe Ruth?" Remember, there really isn't the option for a trade to another team. Who really wants the "Curse of the Bambino" hanging around their necks for the next seventy-odd years? At this point the inveterate baseball fan has an appreciation for why Miller Huggins (Ruth's manager on the Yankees) is also in the Baseball Hall of Fame. I hope the non-sports enthusiast hasn't lost the thread of the business principle.

This is the point when the reader is actually expecting solutions to the dilemmas I've presented. In the first case, I'd consider playing the star at the position where they could really be a star, not where the team temporarily has a need. In the second case, I'd do exactly the same thing because the star needs to perform without limits and hear the applause – but probably should never manage. But it isn't quite so simple, is it? One thing for sure, the executive should be thankful that all the bounty of talent was bestowed on the team, even with the challenges to do something with it. The Yankees figured it out and we are still talking about it eighty years later.

Now, back to the game that my son and I play. It was about the time when he turned twelve that he came up with an innovative compromise to the problem. He started to designate Babe Ruth as his all-time greatest left-handed pitcher. Remember, Ruth also was an outstanding pitcher for the Red Sox before being converted to a daily player – one reason why he may in fact be the greatest player of all-time. I thought that this was an inspired solution and one that may actually have some applicability to the executive faced with a similar problem.

61

Getting the "it"

My first real job managing a staff of people was as the General Manager of WKRQ, a popular FM radio station in Cincinnati. This was at the time when *WKRP in Cincinnati* was a prime time television show. WKRQ was the station used by the Hollywood writers for many of the story lines on the show and provided materials for the set. As a new GM, I couldn't have been wetter behind the ears. It was the classic case of someone who "didn't know what they didn't know." At least I was smart enough to listen to the people around me, which was a key factor to my survival and eventual success. This is a story about one such event from that time in my life.

Early on, I was approached by the leading account executive at the station, Jim Stadtmiller, known affectionately as "Squirrel" (high performing sales reps all have quirky nicknames). He wanted to give me some advice about running the station. His proposal was that we have dinner. I decided it would be a good bonding opportunity. Shortly thereafter, we were together at a well-known restaurant having steaks and sharing small talk right through dessert. Finally, in frustration I said: "Squirrel, you wanted to give me some advice about running the station and so far we haven't talked about that. So, what is your advice?"

Without missing a beat, he replied: "Oh that. Well it's really simple. We need to get the 'it' back." So, I pressed further and asked: "What do you mean? What is the 'it'?" His response will go down as another one of those moments of personal illumination. "I don't know what the 'it' is. But you know it when you have 'it.' And, you know it when you don't. Right now, we don't have 'it.' And, we need to get 'it' back." He was right on target with his comments, as unorthodox as they were. Looking back on the situation, the station's staff must have been terrorized by losing their experienced GM to a promotion, only to be replaced by an unknown "green horn." Before going further, I must alert the reader that two years later WKRQ was named "Radio Station of the Year" by *Billboard Magazine*. I love happy endings, especially ones that are meaningful wins for a leader and a team.

So, I took Squirrel's advice to heart and did a lot of thinking about getting the "it" back. Today, how would I define the "it?" I believe "it" is the spirit that a group of people feel when they are doing something well and when they are also having fun in the process. The spirit keeps feeding on itself as long as the people feel appreciated, challenged and respected by each other. Sometimes this is easily seen in sports teams where the collective talents of the players are enhanced by being subjugated to the overall sense of team. Some teams have "it," and other teams don't.

How do you create the "it?" That could be the topic of another book – maybe one that I'll write someday. I do know where it starts – *by making everyone on a team feel that their contribution is important and necessary.* It keeps going with tangible evidence of success that everyone can claim. You definitely need these "early wins." Then things really take off as soon as success builds upon itself to create further success. The important skill is to keep everyone believing that the team is more important than any single individual.

The next most important thing is to have some fun. The aspect of having fun in one's work is often misunderstood or underappreciated. I'm not talking about staged events like a holiday party where having fun is "required," but might not really be genuine. I'm talking about the little things that people can do for each other day-to-day that make coming to work seem like an adventure, not a punishment. Creating the proper business environment is the key. Then having ways for people to interact and laugh while they are tackling difficult assignments is the challenge.

My friend John Soller, who was the WKRQ GM before me, wrote a memoir and titled it: *Are you having any fun yet?* This is always a great question to ask. We both matured at Taft Broadcasting which had a unique and successful culture based on advancing "having fun" as a key business component. Over twenty years later, the same group of Taft managers gets together on a regular reunion schedule just to celebrate that special culture, and to have a little more fun.

So, ask yourself, does your company or organization have the "it?" How do you know? Well, you know it when you have "it." And, you know it when you don't. If you have to ask someone about this, you probably don't. Now the fun should begin!

62

WHOLEHEARTED ATTENTION FROM SOMEONE WHO BELIEVES IN THEM

I was reading a magazine while on a commercial airline flight, a condition I've experience far too frequently to consider enjoyable. Usually I bring my own fare, from *Sports Illustrated to Kiplinger's.* My reading tastes are fairly predictable and follow typical male interests. I might also mention that I often fall asleep on planes. This has proven to be a godsend in over two million miles strapped to a seat.

On this occasion I was reading a magazine left behind by the previous occupant of the seat. It was one of those "business-chick" magazines which strike me as being filled with self-serving poppycock. Articles in magazines like that tend to focus on "relationships," while I'm more attracted to hard data, statistics and results. Call it gender bias. I'm not saying that a focus on relationships is bad. It's just not my usual "cup of tea."

Wham! There it was – a nugget of information that was destined to change my life (again). The author offered the premise that most problems with relationships at work, with the boss and between peers, could be solved with one simple concept: "Wholehearted attention from someone who believes in them." It was a piece of advice so important that I wrote it down on a scrap of paper and put it into my briefcase (I really didn't want to take the entire magazine). That scrap of paper is still in my briefcase and I have made countless copies for friends, clients and colleagues. Each person I have shared this with has found the power of the message.

Here's what I think it says. Trust is the foundation for interpersonal relationships. Wholehearted attention is a building block toward demonstrating trust. It indicates an overwhelming interest in the well being (the success if you will) of the person receiving the attention. In normal circumstances it feels good to be the recipient of wholehearted attention. The hurdle for the giver is to make the commitment to give it and to be sincere and generous in the process.

Of course, wholehearted attention alone doesn't complete the trust loop. Prisoners get wholehearted attention from prison guards. The loop does close when the giver is genuinely someone who cares about them – and the recipient knows and believes this.

The easiest place to test the formula is in a family setting. Parents, by definition, are always "someone who believes in them (their children)." Problems with relationships, discipline and motivating children generally require more of the "wholehearted attention." A kid knows when this is happening as well as they know when they aren't really on your radar screen. But, spend some quality time with a child and things have a way of improving quickly. That's the great reward to parenting. It also explains why volunteer mentors and organizations like Big Brothers are such powerful forces for good in our society.

Wholehearted attention isn't that difficult to insert into a business situation. The fortunes of the manager are tied to the success of the organization and the individuals who compose the team. Therefore, those being led tend to get ample attention around the metrics of success – or at least they should. But sometimes the more attention being paid, the worse the resulting outcomes become. Perhaps the attention is misplaced or disruptive. But more often, the attention isn't accompanied by the "someone who believes in them" part. Once colleagues sincerely feel this component, all the attention becomes tolerable and quite often has the desired effect of increasing performance.

If you are having trouble believing in the power of this formula, try imagining yourself on the receiving end of it. Would you like your boss to provide you with "wholehearted attention?" And would you like your boss to be someone who "believes in you?" Of course you would.

If it works for you on the receiving end, then find ways for it to work even harder for you on the dispensing side. It is almost a foolproof formula.

63

YOU FIND THE
F%#&ING BASEBALL CAP

This is a story that I love because its point is poignant and universal. All of us have had something happen to us that would be similar. It is also a true story. It was told to me by my good friend Mark Olkowski, one of the finest broadcast engineers around.

The story goes like this. Every year the NBC Television Network carries the Macy's Thanksgiving Day Parade live on the air. It is an enormous undertaking to produce this show out on the streets of New York, with November weather being such a "wild card" every year. As additional background, NBC has a store in 30 Rockefeller Center where anyone can buy merchandise with the NBC "peacock" logo. A few years back, an NBC cameraman was assigned to parade duty with a hand-held street camera. It being a cold day, he wore an NBC baseball cap – one that he purchased for himself at the company store. During the parade, someone in the crowd swiped the ball cap from this cameraman's head. He was powerless to give chase because he was shooting live action. The baseball cap became a parade casualty.

Returning to work the next week the cameraman filled out his expense report for the assignment on Thanksgiving Day – food, incidentals, etc. – as required by management. He submitted this to the accounting department, including a charge and a notation for one "NBC baseball cap" to replace the one that was stolen. In those days the NBC accounting department was known in the industry as being way overstaffed and very picky about withholding expenses (thus justifying their overstaffed existence). The cameraman's expense report ran the gauntlet of the "green eye-shades", resulting in an expense check being cut. But reimbursement for the stolen baseball cap was denied.

Does any of this "Mickey Mouse" bureaucratic behavior start to ring some bells in your mind? Haven't we all been part of some ridiculous story like this?

So, what did the cameraman do? He could have ignored it and gone about his business – one baseball cap to the worse. Instead, he took a different tactic. Because he was often called out on assignments, he had regular opportunities to fill out expense reports. And ever since the day he had his legitimate request denied he has done two things when filling out these expense reports. He has added the cost of one ball cap somewhere - embedded in the report where it can't be traced. Then at the bottom of each expense report he has made the notation, which the accountants at NBC haven't been able to decode: "YFTFBC." It stands for "You Find the F%#&ing Baseball Cap." I don't know how many years this went on. But I'm told it continued for a long time.

The lesson, of course, is to be fair to your employees. And, when it comes to the small stuff, give them the benefit of any doubt. If and when you lose trust over something petty, you run the risk of turning an employee into an adversary, which might ultimately cost you big dollars. Employees (especially union ones, as was the case with the cameraman) are programmed to be skeptical of management. Stories like this one, of a little guy getting even, turn into urban legend (which perhaps the ball cap has become). Your people may not be writing "YFTFBC" on expense reports, but they will certainly be thinking about ways to get back at you if you mess with them over something stupid.

64

THE RELATIVE WORTH OF EACH INDIVIDUAL IS KNOWN BY THE TEAM

I have worked in many organizations, and I've provided consulting for many others. The observation above is universal to all the organizations that I've been a part of from businesses to non-profits. I keep looking for exceptions to this rule, but so far I haven't found any.

When you work with a group of individuals, just like when you play on an athletic team, the talents, skills and proclivities of each person are relatively well-understood over time. New organizations and teams struggle with this very issue as they try to grow and become more efficient and effective. It is in everyone's interest to accelerate the process for "better results faster" (to borrow the tag line form PrimeGenesis, partners of mine who focus on on-boarding new executives). All people in work, or quasi-work, situations evaluate their peers. It is a mistake of massive proportions to believe this doesn't happen.

We can all point to situations to illustrate the point. In every venture (public or private) the actual compensation details are almost always known by everyone working with, or near, other employees. There is an insatiable desire to know one's relative worth, especially against others that a person evaluates on their internal scale against personal performance (which might be totally delusional). Unfortunately, there is also a tendency in HR departments for clerks to be less than tight-lipped or indiscreet enough to allow important personel information be "found on the copy machine." Quite often, employees announce to each other their "deals" in order to compare notes. At the highest levels, compensation in public companies is a matter of record, easy to find and interpret. It is a "given" that the people you work with know your exact compensation or can make a close enough guess for "government work." If you want to test this, simply write down the names of the people you work closely with and try to attach a compensation number to them. This isn't hard to do. So why believe that the people around you aren't doing it?

Compensation doesn't always measure relative worth. The son or daughter of the boss tends to make more money than they deserve. No surprises here. There are also anomalies in organizations based on time, grade and favoritism. Organizations and businesses aren't perfect and merit isn't always correlated accurately to pay. If you are on the short end of a discrepancy I'm not sure what advice to provide – except perhaps to ignore it for your own sanity. If you do your job well and you are valuable, compensation tends to follow performance over time. If it doesn't, simply change jobs and become valuable to some other organization.

The more insidious condition exists in an organization when everyone knows who does a good job and also who the proverbial "gold bricks" are. The health of a high-performance organization actually depends on the ability of the leader to identify the laggards and get rid of them. Letting them survive and provide continued contrast to the stated goals of the organization is the equivalent of encouraging a cancer to grow. Cut it out. The test of who qualifies is easy. When you have a hard job to do, who do you seek out to do it, especially if it reflects on your success? The people you avoid, the ones you don't trust, are the laggards.

In a similar vein, executives shouldn't be hesitant to pay higher comp and bonuses (and by this I mean much higher) to the stars that make an extraordinary contribution. This is precisely the attraction to many players that gravitate toward selling. They like the notion that they are measured by performance and not "capped" in the amount of money they can make. The thinking should also apply to star performers in the rank-in-file.

I'm reminded of the story of Bill Veeck (author of *Veeck, as in Wreck*) who was an executive at a couple major league baseball teams during his career. He said (and I may be paraphrasing here): "It's not the high cost of my star players that troubles me, it's the high cost of mediocrity." This is so easy to understand in baseball, but harder to implement in our own business situations.

It is a good rule of thumb to suppose that everyone knows who is doing the work and that everyone knows what people are being paid. The successful executive matches-up this information such that the team can be successful because there isn't economic disparity.

You know you haven't got it figured out when people you like, and need, start leaving. Tough way to learn the lesson. Reading this chapter is meant to be easier!

65

CHANGE THE PERSON IN
THIRTY DAYS

Anyone who has ever managed a group of managers, each of whom is responsible for a team of people, has come face to face with a predictable challenge. At some point, one of the managers and the team will start to underperform. Upon further inspection it will be obvious to you that the reason for the shortfall in performance is substandard performance by one or more members of the underperforming team. The manager of that team might even have come to the same realization. This becomes unavoidable after his or her performance is called into question. Then the tendency is to dig deeper into the organization looking for answers. But the stage is set. Now you know, and your manager knows, that there are performance gaps inside the team. There must be changes to stem the downward slide of the team and to reverse fortunes back toward improvement.

So, what do you do? The executive should immediately gravitate toward making the necessary personnel changes to get things fixed. The executive should be most cognizant of the sense of urgency to turn things around. One of the best measures of executive upward mobility is the tendency to attack known problems swiftly. And why not? So, the executive approaches his manager with the problem looking for a partner to implement a solution. But, the manager might well "whiff" at this pitch. Now the executive has another problem.

The scenario plays out in a predictable fashion. Only the names and characters change slightly, case to case. The manager makes an impassioned pitch not to dismiss the underperforming person(s), but instead to give them one last chance at improvement. It is a point of view with some merit. The cost is high for having downtime and to recruit a replacement. Perhaps there is expense, like severance (I always find it ironic when companies reward underperformers to leave), to untangle the poor performer from the organization. Add to the equation the realization that at various times everyone can have distractions that affect performance at work – health problems, family issues, etc. Employers don't want to appear insensitive to their employees. They believe, correctly, that everyone is watching and jeopardizing the culture of "trust" that has been established is dangerous. So, your manager is probably doing you a favor by slowing you down and petitioning for more time to evaluate the situation.

Behind the scenes is a laundry list of other reasons for the manager to suggest this course of action. They may be afraid of the process of terminating the weak person, which often turns ugly. Perhaps they have an outside relationship with this person and there might be genuine affection between them that transcends work. They may be concerned with the process of actually replacing one person with another. This comes in a couple of flavors. With an employee off the team, the team is playing shorthanded and results will reflect that. A bonus may be in jeopardy. By hiring a new person, the performance measures may not change quickly enough, or at all. So, managers cling to the "devil they know." The most insidious of the explanations is that the manager feels that with a change in the team there is no longer a culprit to blame and future shortfalls in performance will reflect directly back on him or her, putting their job in jeopardy.

For all of these reasons, organizational and personal, it is the classic response of a manager to ask for more time to evaluate the situation. Notice that this is a passive activity. More time to evaluate a situation really doesn't address the problem. At best, some new data take the heat off the manager to actually do anything and life continues in the comfortable ruts that have become entrenched. At worst, conditions deteriorate further.

Good executives see the situation for what it is – a passive delaying tactic. I've seen more than a few toss their hands in frustration. Their leadership is being tested and undoubtedly someone higher in the organization is looking to them to implement a solution.

Here is a suggestion. It is one that I have tried myself many times with very good results. Grant the line manager his request for more time on behalf of the problem employee. But convert the exercise from being passive to becoming active. My technique was to tell the manager to: *"Change the person in thirty days, or change the person in thirty days."* The first "change the person" refers to a behavioral change for the person creating the problem. This is through some active intervention on the manager's part with defined benchmarks for improvement, including a permanent change in attitude if necessary. Now the manager is actively engaged in the process and takes ownership for the success of the plan he originally suggested. Sometimes the results are surprisingly good. Mission accomplished.

But, sometimes even the manager knows that the cause is already lost and it is easier to buy more time than it is to fix the problem. Now comes the second "change the person." This refers to actually making a personnel change, a new person for the old person. With the timeframe of thirty days there can be no delays in addressing the problem head-on with the troubled employee. The manager will make a decision about the long-term prospects much earlier into the process. No matter what, the manager should start interviewing for replacements based on the acknowledged probability that the incumbent employee may not survive. Even if a new person isn't hired, the process of looking for new blood has value, if only to have immediate options if something else adverse happens to the team. You could make the case that managers should always be looking for people to improve their teams.

If your manager doesn't rise to the challenge to "Change the person in thirty days, or change the person in thirty days" there are bigger problems. As the executive, you must now take your own advice and "Change the person in thirty days, or change the person in thirty days." This caps the solution cycle at sixty days. If you don't follow this advice be hopeful that your boss hasn't read this chapter.

66

CUT HARD, CUT DEEP
AND CUT ONCE

Every executive eventually has to face the prospect of making cuts in the size of the overall workforce at some point in their career. This may be to effect radical change in the culture of an organization that has grown sluggish or diseased over time. Sometimes entire businesses or divisions need to be amputated. Perhaps the level of business activity requires that cuts have to be made to keep expenses aligned with anticipated revenues. Making subtractions to the employee roster is every bit as common as making additions. Making additions is more fun. Making cuts is painful for all concerned.

This pain cuts across both the management and the employee ranks. I'm not sure who endures the most. You can cut the stress with a dull knife. Once the decision has been made to reduce the workforce, there is only one plan for the execution of the decision that limits the stress and the residual damage. Cut hard, cut deep and cut once.

The reason that some executives don't follow this advice is that they believe that if they only make minimal cuts, there may be a sudden business reversal that will save the day and thus the need for further cuts. Elsewhere in this book we discuss the flawed logic of believing in "silver bullet" solutions to instantaneously reverse business fortunes. This isn't likely to happen.

Actually, there is more logic in cutting deeply – even deeper than what might be necessary at the specific moment in time. If you cut deep and things get worse, at least you have anticipated the worst case and stopped further bleeding. But, if you cut deep and things get better, what's the worst case that you are facing? You go out and add employees, an event with positive consequences and momentum for the business. The business goal is to keep the number of negative events to a minimum.

The absolute worst case is to have a business spiral down through a steady drumbeat of cut after cut after cut. The process of progressive cuts makes a bad decision (to wait) even worse. People wonder if they are in the next wave of cuts. The employees you need the most start looking for alternative jobs. The very best find them. The manager in charge has a constantly negative cloud hanging over the business that makes it much more difficult to accomplish anything at the time when maximum attention is needed. This speaks to the benefit of making one definitive cut. At least everyone in the organization can start healing and the outlook has the chance of turning positive if the perception is "the worst is over."

67

EMPLOYEES ARE ARMED
AND DANGEROUS

There is a reluctance to subtract employees in an organization that is the outgrowth of a collective body of experience shared by executives, managers and HR specialists alike. I'm about to add to this collective experience. Simply stated, be careful because employees are armed and dangerous (to the health and financial well-being of the organization). Their weapon of choice is the legal profession.

Stories illuminate the truth. Here is one of mine. Many years ago when I was a COO, our company acquired a business unit as part of a larger transaction. Within this unit were a number of senior executives. It was readily apparent that there was a redundancy in job responsibilities that begged for correction. In one particular case the employee was given three months of job time and three months of severance to find a new position outside the company – a total of six months. This was very generous by industry measures. The employee willingly accepted this offer and signed a severance agreement. Essentially, she performed no additional work for the company. We were comfortable with that because we were concerned that her time be used to find new employment, with our endorsement. Unfortunately, she was unable to land a new job within the timeframe (and really didn't try too hard). She separated from the company on the pre-agreed timetable. Within days our company was handed a lawsuit for discrimination based on age and gender. This was a disappointing surprise because all through the process we were supportive and positive in our recommendations for this person.

Then the story really turned bizarre. One of the industry trade journals called me about the lawsuit. I was correctly advised not to talk about the specific case or the specific individual. To deflect questions that were being asked, I simply commented that: "We lived in a world where anyone can hire a polyester lawyer with a night school degree and sue somebody." I thought I was being clever. Many fellow industry leaders called me to share a good laugh at that comment. A few days later the lawyer for the employee (remember, nobody was ever identified by name) sued the company, and me personally, for "defamation of character." If it hadn't happened to me, this might have been funny. It is the only time in my life that I have been personally threatened with legal action. In the end, because the business unit was resold to a third party, our company paid a good-sized settlement to make this frivolous suit disappear before the closing. The bad guys won.

Arming employees with lawyers makes every working person dangerous to the organization. There is precious little cover in the laws of most states. My experience has been that you never want to take an employee dispute to court, especially to a jury. The average person in a jury box is cheering for the little guy to figuratively "win the lottery" by extracting money from "big business." My own mother actually is conditioned to think along these lines. She understands that I support the honest interests of business. She just can't help herself. So, why would anybody think that justice will be served with a jury stacked by well-meaning people like my own mother?

Good laws are good for business. And good lawyers are necessary to keep businesses honest. But in a world of too many lawyers per capita, the average worker now has the firepower of an assault weapon and the comparisons to holding up a 7-Eleven Store aren't too far-fetched.

In response, executives and managers are loathe to hire somebody (they might eventually have to fire) or to fire somebody (that they probably shouldn't have hired or kept on in the first instance). The condition tends to perpetuate a culture of mediocrity – which is contrary to high performance.

What are the possible remedies? The most obvious one is to not break the law regarding employees. This is always a good piece of advice. The next guidance is to be very careful in the hiring process. Remember, here again, you make money when you buy. The cost of a failed employee is compounded by a financially messy exit. Watch for the tell-tale signs in the interview and referencing process. Large gaps in a resume are warning lights. So are bland responses from references. In today's culture it is dangerous to be negative, so neutral is the modern-day equivalent. Asking an applicant about the circumstances of their most recent position that has them motivated to seek alternative employment can provide revealing windows into core character traits. If they are married to a lawyer, or have a close family member negotiating on their behalf, you might want to be extra careful.

Remember that employees, like all costs, are an investment in revenue. If there isn't a return on the investment, make a change. Do it sooner rather than later. How you do it is important and can often mitigate unnecessary damage. But, executives are charged with the responsibility of adding value, not with conducting jobs programs.

One final reflection. I actually fired a person in his office who was hung over and had a number of hunting rifles stacked against the wall. Talk about armed and dangerous! That is a story for another book.

68

SHIRTSLEEVES TO SHIRTSLEEVES IN THREE GENERATIONS

This is a favorite saying of my mother. Many people have used this adage, or something similar, to describe the phenomenon of family money disappearing in three generations. It wouldn't keep being repeated if there weren't some degree of truth to it. We all know wealthy individuals who haven't worked for their money and seem to have no difficulty in spending it. This is the notion of "making a small fortune" by starting with "a large one." But, I believe the adage holds meaningful lessons for family-owned businesses, which is why I've included it.

Allow me to make a clear and forceful case in favor of family-owned businesses. I wish I had been able to start one, or I had inherited one. Underlying every family business is at least one entrepreneurial person with determination and self-sacrifice. Every business was once a small business, including large multi-national corporations. A preponderance of today's successful corporations started as family-owned businesses – even if today that legacy is all but invisible. So, I believe that the small, family-owned business is the cornerstone of America and should be celebrated.

If only I had been smart enough to start my own business early enough in my career. That's the lament of many senior executives after they have been battered and bloodied in the Cuisinart of corporate existence. In addition to the fulfillment of seeing something begin as a seed and grow to a profitable enterprise, there are wonderful family opportunities that success can provide. Having family members, especially sons and daughters, join in the development of a business is very fulfilling. It means that loved ones are usually close to home and that relationships are able to evolve for a lifetime. It is every parent's dream. There are added opportunities for wealth management and transference that the average executive isn't able to take advantage of. Yes, family businesses are special.

But family-owned, or controlled, businesses may be terrible investments for the outsider, and over time they tend to be frustrating places to work for the aggressive and entrepreneurial executive.

On the investment side, it is impossible to safeguard against the tendency of the family owners to "tune" the business toward advantages to the family. Any of us would do the same if we were in the same situation. So, it shouldn't be hard to imagine that it happens and that it is pervasive. This tendency is illuminated when you are purchasing a family business. The financial data have to be reformatted into a pro-forma resembling standard business practice. What shakes out is stuff like non-working family members on the payroll, excessive automobiles and perks (including indiscriminate use of corporate aircraft), funny bonuses and incentives, and a host of manipulations designed to avoid (for a time) the payment of taxes. All of these are detrimental to the outside, third-party investor with a minority position. There are lots of opportunities to invest with honest accounting and shareholder-focused management. Why make this investment choice?

The bigger pothole to avoid could be working for a family business long-term. A self-respecting executive with a fastball can become frustrated. I say this as harsh self-criticism. I've done this myself and really only learned the lesson after the third time. Again, the pattern of prejudice is easy to predict – even when you are being well paid, which is commonly the incentive that turns your head.

Here's the worst scenario. "Senior" made the business successful and does just about as he or she pleases to run things with their personal interests front and center, often just on the blurry fringe of good accounting practice. "Junior" (generically – but it could be any family member genetically) doesn't have to play by the same rules as everyone else. As someone once told me: "He was born on third base, and he thinks he hit a triple." And unless there is some bolstering of the gene pool from the outside, Junior may not have the determination or the appetite for self-sacrifice that Senior had (or once had). All the downside of doing the heavy lifting is pushed down to the hired help. When things go bad, as they are apt to do under the circumstances, who do you think takes the first abuse? And, there is no upside leverage for sustainable financial rewards unless you marry into the family. Their "game within a game" becomes one of trying to provide an annuity for as many family members and generations as possible.

This is all wonderful if you are one of the insiders. This can be misery if you aren't. It is no wonder that ultimately a family business is challenged to keep the urgency and the focus needed to extend beyond three generations. In a world of high velocity challenges, it will be hard to successfully manage beyond two generations. Three generations requires somebody rolling up their shirtsleeves.

SECTION IX
ACCOUNTING WISE

69

THE NUMBERS ONLY ADD
AND SUBTRACT ONE WAY

I have a friend named Marty who was the CEO of a TV station partnership assembled in the late 1980's when the prices for TV stations were at historic highs. The company didn't do very well over the next few years when broadcasting revenues slowed down but the burden of interest on borrowed money didn't. The company was finally liquidated in the mid-90's, with many of the stations selling at a loss from their initial purchase prices. It wasn't a happy story or a time for my friend to feign being a business genius. Knowing that Marty had probably learned a lot in this process I asked him over lunch one day for the most important lesson he learned. He didn't hesitate. "I learned that the math is the math and that numbers only add and subtract one way."

Of course he was right, at least about the simple truth that we all learn in grade school. But his point, and his experience, pointed to a much deeper truth – one worth exploring.

Be careful when you analyze a business. Every one is slightly different. But they all have key "drivers" for the inputs that you will record as operational revenues and expenses. I like to do simple "back of envelope" models when I first analyze a business, just to try to capture these drivers. Later, a larger and more comprehensive model can be assembled. This isn't brain surgery to be sure. Learn to know where the numbers come from that are called revenues and how expenses appear. Then it is important to understand all the multiple "drivers" of the business equation and how they work together.

Here is where the mistake often takes place in the analysis and where Marty made his mistake. Once the drivers are identified, then "assumptions" are placed into the equations to deliver a unified picture of the business. Every single one of the assumptions has its own unique probability equation, ranging from unreasonably negative to unreasonably positive. In other words, each assumption has its own "bell curve" of likely results. The most likely are at the center of the bell curve and the most unlikely are at the fringes, by a multiple of standard deviations.

Inserting assumptions into a business model is totally dependent on the viewpoint of the person controlling the model. Putting all the mini-bell curves for assumptions together into the overall model creates a bell curve for the whole. Now for the pertinent question. Does the business analyst want to find the range of likely outcomes for the business? Or, do they want to find the most optimistic scenario to lure investors with more money than common sense? The folks in the business of raising money have incentives to position the company in the most positive light. Mathematically, this isn't so hard if you just look toward the most optimistic sides of the bell curves for each of the assumptions. This is the statistical equivalent of picking winners for every race on the card at a thoroughbred track. Yes, it is possible for this to happen. But, it is not probable! Of course, the end result is that the true bell curve for the business isn't presented at all. Buyer beware.

So, this was what my friend Marty was really telling me. When you add and subtract, and more importantly when you multiply the numbers, they can only provide you a result as good as the true ranges for each of the assumptions that are used. You can make a case for practically anything, even a wildly optimistic outcome, if that is the goal. On the other hand, the real probability is that each of the data points is going to hover near the center of their own particular bell curve and the ultimate historical result must be served by the fundamental resulting math. "The math is the math."

70

IT'S NOT THE FIGURES THAT LIE

It's not the figures that lie. *It's the liars that figure.* This adage has been around for a long time, but never has it been more pertinent to the executive. One only has to think about Enron and the consequences of the resulting oversight regulations promulgated by Sarbanes-Oxley to grasp the point.

Accounting is a process of recording data. We tend to believe numbers that are placed logically on a sheet of paper and that add and subtract accurately. Accounting standards are a safeguard from unseemly practices by the people in charge of assembling the numbers. So, over time we've developed a level of trust for the data we get in an officially sanctioned manner. Add the wizardry of computers and we actually start to believe that the numbers are near perfectly accurate. This is ironic to anyone who has ever worked with computer software because "glitches" abound. And there is the reality of "garbage in – garbage out."

Managers beware. Through a combination of brow-beating people internally to make projections and putting a "smiley face" on all external communications, the corporate culture puts accounting departments between the jaws of a vise. As a coping technique, they learn to gravitate toward shades of grey that are the most favorable and acceptable for short-term job security. Sometimes the complexity of the situation and the vagaries of software are accomplices to obfuscating the truth.

Managers need good and accurate information to make intelligent business decisions. Executives wouldn't disagree with that statement. The logical behavior would be to reward "truth-telling." It all works smoothly as long as the information is favorable and the company is doing well. But, a condition of perpetually "blue skies" is an unrealistic expectation for an organization over extended time horizons. Invariably, there will be ups and downs. Managers hate this, especially when it happens inside their direct organization and even more particularly when their compensation is tied to the beat of steadily positive results. So, in an attempt to "smooth" results, adjustments are sought out to make reported results actually mirror the expectations of all audiences that appreciate predictability.

What are the executive "take-aways" from this very common vulnerability? The first is that an executive should never really trust the veracity of data that is submitted to them. It is important that data and numbers be inspected. At some point, the organization expects that to be done. Moreover, the organization expects the executive to own the numbers. As I challenge the executives that I coach: "Have command of your data." It is a fundamental expectation for leaders in business. Not having command of the data is a "hanging offense."

The second observation is to nurture an internal culture of truth. The trust between executive teams is the lubrication that actually makes the accomplishment of goals possible. Take the trust away and then the friction starts to slow the operation down and a breakdown of some magnitude is inevitable. In simplest terms, don't tolerate any liars – especially if they are in the business of figuring.

71

EXPENSES ARE
INVESTMENTS IN REVENUE

This one harkens back to my days at Clear Channel Communications and was a favorite reminder of Mark Mays, who probably learned it from another source.

Again, it is simple in concept, but profound and complicated in the application.

The foundation for all enterprises (including non-profits) is to manage revenues (inflow) against expenses (outflow). If you are supposed to make money, then the goal is to have profits. If you aren't chartered to make money, the goal is only slightly different, to get the most value in return for a structured "break even."

A rational investor or executive wouldn't start a business unless there was at least the prospect of earning a profit or creating value – something to show for time and treasury invested. Even a public interest project wouldn't get sustained support unless the social benefits for serving the clients were in alignment, and hopefully very effective, against the hard cost (public or private) of providing the service.

But investors and executives aren't always rational. They get the concept. In fact, there is a good argument that they always get the concept. This is because they selectively employ the concept for their personal equation (by spending irrationally on expenses to keep a job, along with the benefits) versus looking at the overall health of the enterprise.

Mistakes are made in daily practice. Budgets are spent in the final quarter or month, often for non-essential items, rather than turn the money back to the company or organization. This is a systemic violation of the principle. Yet, I hardly know a manager or organization that doesn't engage in some variation of this misguided thinking. If the money is there, spend it!

One of the most useful times to be reminded of the principle is when budgets are actually being formulated for a new fiscal year. It is amazing how detailed and seemingly accurate most managers can come in identifying expenses. It is the rare executive that marries increases in expenses with matching increases (with appropriate margins) in revenue. This is why the budgeting process becomes a cat-and-mouse game at many organizations.

When you actually own your own business you become acutely aware of expenses being investments in revenue. The light of day is harsh. There is every incentive to be thorough in the analysis. But still, there is an institutionalized process that causes many business owners to act irrationally. The catalyst for this is taxation. Business owners go through extreme contortions just to save some taxes? Sometimes it makes sense because a benefit can be diverted to your family (say by providing a summer job to a child). Other times it can be just plain foolish (like buying a Hummer as a company car).

In larger companies there is almost always an opportunity to apply this rule and look like a hero. Isn't this the simple explanation for the success of notable executives like Jack Welch? Inserting this culture into the heart and soul of an organization can have powerful results. Getting there can be quite the challenge. You may need better data to measure. Or, you may need some "public hangings" in order to convince the organization that there has been a change in cultural inertia.

Large or small, public or private, for profit or non-profit, thinking of expenses as investments is a good starting point for squeezing more out of the cost-benefit equation - the universal benchmark for success.

72

You don't get
what you don't pay for

You've heard the old saying: "You get what you pay for." It has been carried on from generation to generation because it captures a universal truth – at least to some degree. But is it precise? My father didn't think so. So, he changed the wording in a clever way that I believe is actually more accurate: "You don't get what you don't pay for."

Think about it. Do you always get what you pay for? The truth is that you don't. In consumer transactions, some come close – say, money for a gallon of milk. Here, assuming that the milk isn't spoiled, you actually do get what you pay for. In other words, your expectations are met and the transaction is a fair one in your mind. But consider the case of an invisible service like a car repair. Unless you are there to watch the repair being made with a stop watch and then audit the parts replaced, it is hard to know if what you are paying is a fair price for a fair value. But, you do know one thing. If you don't pay for something, or you don't pay enough, there isn't any chance that the repair will be made correctly. You are never sure that you got what you paid for. But you do know that you'll never get what you didn't pay for. That was my father's observation.

So, what practical behavioral change can you take away from this observation – one that will either make or save you money? Right up front, I'll admit that this is a tough one to manage. So many aspects of our lives are engaged with product and service providers where the actual benefit is elusive. Sometimes this is because the benefit is in the future, like with investment planning advice. How do you really know if you got what you paid for until after the data is collected? You don't. But, you are conditioned to operate on the premise that you won't get what you don't pay for. Thus the tendency to make future investment decisions with those advisors having a track record in the past tense. Or more striking, there is the notion that if you pay an investment advisor a hefty fee then the advisor must be better than average and his advice will yield superior future results. We know this isn't statistically true, but we can't help ourselves from believing the myth. Success stories, like that of Warren Buffet, keep us believing in the magical powers of a savant.

So, common sense is the first line of defense for trying to get what you pay for. The next line of defense is inspection. If you actually watched the auto mechanic fix your car and allowed for him to make a legitimate profit on the cost of parts, you would be adequately prepared to assess if the job was done at a fair price. So much of business integrity is compromised by the fact that vendors really won't let the consumer make an assessment of fair value, especially for services. They charge what they think the individual customer or the market can bear. It isn't only car mechanics that indulge in this chicanery (for the record, I happen to have an honest car mechanic). Professionals – like lawyers – are expert at it. If you really checked their actual time spent against their billing logs you might discover that they are able to bill for upwards of 150% of their time – a statistical miracle.

This last example points to the likely first response by a vendor when you think you have overpaid; "You shouldn't measure the time, but measure the result." Is it worth the money to have your car fixed? Is it worth the money to have the legal matter addressed? Then, consumer, you shouldn't actually worry about the time spent and how the bill was prepared. This is the classic "switch pitch" when the process of doing the inspection makes the vendor nervous. The argument would be OK if you actually agreed in advance to pay $X for Y services. But some vendors work on the premise that they can manipulate the system from both ends. Again, this points to the wisdom of my father's observation.

The providers of goods and services should take note. Consumers aren't perpetually stupid. Eventually they come to the same conclusion as my dad. Someone with a better idea comes along. From the supply side there emerge tremendous opportunities to set up businesses as the exceptions to the rule. It really isn't difficult to understand the pricing at Jiffy Lube, or at H&R Block – or their success. How many service stations (I hate to keep picking on them, but the illustration is instructive) now advertise in "penny savers" with a discount coupon for oil changes, below what Jiffy Lube charges? They once owned this category of easy maintenance, until they became an industry perceived to be on the wrong side of the integrity curve.

As a final thought, if you think my father didn't have it right, ask yourself this: Are you getting full value for what you pay in taxes to the Government? Of course not. You certainly don't get what you pay for (except if you are a person with needs paying nothing and eligible for a subsidy). But the entire system of taxation (from the viewpoint of the actual taxpayers – a minority of the population) is built on the premise that the people paying taxes don't get what they don't pay for.

73

Hindsight is 20/20

"But, hindsight is 20/20." How many times have you heard this off-hand observation recited to you? It usually comes with a bit of an attitude, as if someone is invisibly wagging their index finger when they deliver the message. The intent is to remind the recipient that the past can't be changed and the future can't be predicted on the basis of past events, even if they are understood with perfectly clarity. The phrase is almost always invoked to cover a past mistake that would have been corrected had attention been paid at the time key decisions were made or, ironically, if there had been better data to make decisions. It is a bit like seeking absolution for sins by going to confession with the overtone that the past is the past and now it can't be changed. So, the listener is being chided to move on to thinking about the future, and to quit worrying about the past. While this advice may be correct in theology, it is a misguided notion in business.

Let's break it down. If you have "20/20 hindsight," presumably you have excellent data about what went on, and why. *This is valuable information.* It is much too valuable to be tossed aside with the admonition to start building the future from scratch, forgetting about the past. Indeed, the more current the data are, the more valuable its decision-making influence is to the manager or the executive. The idea that it is too late to change past decisions is equally flawed. Similar decisions are very likely to appear again and again, perhaps with a little cosmetic "make-up" to disguise them. Even if the history is "ancient" in business cycle terms (a year or two), there are still good lessons to be learned and behaviors to be modified for better future results.

If you were to assume that available data on the operations of a business (pick the category: sales, customer satisfaction, margins, returns, retention, etc.) are accurate as of yesterday, then *the predictive value of that same data for tomorrow is actually incredibly high.* High-performance business cultures strive for high velocity in data for just this reason. They know that they might be able to correct for bad decisions more rapidly, as opposed to making the same bad decisions over and over due to neglect.

The value of data does fall off at the shoulders, by the calendar passage of time in two ways. As the data ages, they become less accurate as an immediate future predictor. And, as current data are projected further out into the future, they become less accurate because new variables in the future have a way of independently affecting and disrupting things. But yesterday's data are incredibly valuable and extraordinarily accurate toward predicting tomorrow's results. Period to period comparisons (like April 2007 to April 2008) have the added benefit of equalizing for seasonal anomalies.

"Hindsight" is actually a great and necessary tool for the thoughtful manager. There is real power in being able to correct a bad decision – not yesterday's decision, but possibly tomorrow's. It is one reason why very successful leaders are always searching for more and better performance measures.

The backside of the equation is also instructive. When weaker managers and key contributors reject past data and performance measures, it is usually because the direction of their future (as measured by the past) is flat, or may be declining. And even if the trend line is advancing, underachievers have an inherent fear that success might be unsustainable. Some just hate admitting that they were wrong in the past, which is the first step required to change behavior. Their cover story is that "hindsight is 20/20." So, forget about it.

Next time someone wags that figurative finger at you, it might be interesting to take a harder look at the messenger. The ability to tap fresh and accurate data is always great news, willingly embraced by successful leaders and executives eager to improve decision making.

Hindsight is 20/20. I say "Hallelujah!"

SECTION X
COMMUNICATION WISE

74

THE SMARTEST PERSON
IN THE ROOM
USUALLY SAYS THE LEAST

The smartest person in any official meeting usually has the least to say, at least at the outset. Unfortunately, sometimes the dumbest person also says very little. For those keeping score, it can be confusing.

So much of our learned behavior is patterned to project authority, to control or to dominate. You see it all the time in business behavior. It really shouldn't be all that surprising, since it is prevalent and institutionalized throughout the many years of formal education that we all endure. Having the right answer pleases the teacher. Being smart leads to advancement and opportunity. Proving that you are smarter is a game that smart people learn the rules for and at which they become proficient. Making presentations is coached. Speaking up at meetings is encouraged, even expected. Personally taking credit for ideas and results, sometimes beyond objective reality, is tolerated. In a world where parents reportedly struggle to get their children into the right nursery school as a glide path for success, the rules and the behavior of self-promotion become all the more exaggerated.

Yet, it has been my observation that some of the smartest people I've ever met don't say very much at meetings – at least not at first. The fundamental reason for this is that they are intent on listening. "You can observe a lot by just watching." Yogi Berra had it right. It is actually much harder to listen and observe when you are also speaking to impress. It isn't dissimilar from driving a car while using your portable phone. There just isn't enough bandwidth for timesharing in the human brain, even in the above-average ones.

So, let's make the point again that listening is important. One of the best lines I've heard as an executive coach was from a fellow who hired lots of middle managers. He said it simply: "I tell them (my new hires) to hit the ground listening." Notice, he didn't say, running or talking. This is great insight and advice for all executives.

It's not that the smart people should remain silent in meetings or high-level conversations. They all eventually speak. When they do, people tend to listen with more attention. Here's why. The smart person has been processing information, and more of it, by keeping silent early in the dialog. He or she gets the benefit of all the viewpoints that emerge, not just the ones they think of themselves. And here's the magic. They are able to select the essential information and arguments and then reprocess them for the others in the meeting. That's the skill that is the mark of the truly talented leader. Much of it will sound familiar, and quite brilliant, because at least one other person in the room already agrees with it. So, the business skill to develop isn't the same one we are rewarded for as children. The skill is to separate the valuable data and ideas from the irrelevant and then to repackage them in a manner that is digestible by the others that need to be converted into some sort of action. This could be a brick in the foundation of a pretty good definition of leadership. Part of the skill is weaving threads of consensus, also useful in most cases. Part of it is understanding that, unlike in school, there often isn't one clear and definitive answer to a business challenge. The goal isn't to prove you are smart. The goal is to get something positive accomplished. That makes you smart.

The really smart school children eventually understand that the other students don't like or trust the smartest people in class. The teacher's pet is roundly despised. They have to adjust their personal behavior to succeed and become effective in the real world. That's my experience, anyway.

75

Don't believe
your own bullshit

One of my friends suggested that the title of this chapter should have been the title of this book. He cites two reasons for this. First, it encompasses many of the large and small sins that managers commit. Second, it is an outrageous statement that is sure to attract some attention – especially on the crowded shelves of a bookseller where every author is vying for attention and uses outrageous titles.

This is another one of the great delusions in business. Namely, that if you say something often enough, and you really believe it, then it will come true. It is a seductive trap to fall into.

In business, like life, if you don't believe in what you are doing then the act of doing it becomes unfulfilling and difficult. Sometimes this lack of fulfillment is overcome by compensation. We all know people who will do almost anything for money. If money isn't the answer, then it is likely that a person will try to overcome or escape their frustration, if they can. It is particularly important for the manager, as the leader of a team, to project a positive aura around the business proposition at hand. It keeps his or her attitude in the proper mindset. More importantly, it projects confidence to the rest of the team. In short, the team will be only able to salute the flag if the leader is convincing. Leaders adopt the persona of being convincing. Some call it charisma.

There is an extension of this mindset pertaining to communication to stakeholders. Again, if the folks running the show aren't convinced of the efficacy of doing something, this will have a negative influence on the others that are investing their time and money.

So, senior managers, and especially CEOs are in a box. The dilemma is that no matter what happens, it is incumbent upon them to be positive and to project success. If they don't, the consequences are dire - among the employees, to the stakeholders and to them personally.

The mistake is to make positive news about a company seem much bigger and more consequential that it probably is in reality. This is especially true in very large corporations where actually moving a stock $1 on a public exchange can add hundreds of millions in enterprise value. Small movements in the stock price can have tremendous value consequences. A steady drumbeat of good news can really accelerate the worth of a company and the personal worth of individuals in the company, many of whom are holding valuable stock options.

It isn't wrong to tell the overall market about good news. In fact there are requirements to divulge any news (good or bad) if it is material, a standard that is a matter of discretion for the management of a company. There are even some well-known executives who have had a string of jobs based on their abilities to tell good stories about their companies, often well ahead of any measurable results.

Is it wrong for leaders to take the positive view of things when reporting to their staff and stakeholders? It might be, depending on how wildly optimistic a story is created. Or, it could be perfectly fine because the news is within a reasonable range. Of course, the box gets tighter, like being squeezed by a vise, if the real news about the enterprise isn't positive. Worse yet, if it is downright discouraging. Then painting a "fairly tale" picture is unfair to all concerned.

But none of this is actually the central point of this chapter – just the background. The point is that *the manager shouldn't ever completely believe the stories that he is telling to the outside world.* He or she should constantly strive to find the truth, since it is only working with the truth that a leader can determine a direction and strategy to move forward. Even if the manager is telling the outside about the most optimistic scenarios, the manager should be passionate about really knowing where the enterprise is on the playing field. It is only by knowing this that a plan for progress can be made. So, don't get caught in the grand delusion of actually believing what you are communicating. The challenge for a good manager is to seek the truth and to improve upon it.

Of course, this touches on another delusion in business – which assumes that executives, managers and investors really want to know the truth. But, I'll save that one for another book. Hint – they probably don't.

76

BUSINESS IS A
CONTACT SPORT

Do you enjoy a clever play on words? This chapter's title allows me to address two important subjects under the very same heading.

The traditional view of contact sports is one where players physically bump into one another in order to establish position and create an advantage. I've yet to observe a physical confrontation in business, although a couple of times it has been close. There is a fair amount of figurative bumping, jousting and jockeying for position. You have to expect it. You have to deal with it. You almost have to like it to succeed. Some of it is overt and brutal, while some is subtle and brutal. But, succeeding in business as an executive implies that you must find a way to succeed, given the rules of the game. The rules don't change and complaining about the rules is a waste of productive time.

But business is also a contact sport in a completely different way. It relies on human interaction. It depends on the figurative contact and the communication between people. Commerce is by definition the exchange of goods and services in the marketplace. There are providers, consumers and brokers in between the two groups. But successful human interaction is required for the system to work.

As a subset of this thought, business relies on "contacts" in the colloquial definition. It relies on the people you know and the people who know you. This subject has even has its very own verb "network." All of us in business are very aware of our network of contacts. We network every day. And there is a constant need to do "networking" in business.

This is the part I like best in wordsmithing, when there is symmetry and convergence in two seemingly unrelated concepts (all starting with the metaphor of business being a contact sport). Think of every person you meet as having a positive or a negative charge after you bump into them in business (contact sport #1). In large measure, you determine this charge – positive or negative. Now consider this. Only the people with positive charges are actually candidates for being contacts (contact sport #2) in the future. You'll have to work the list and build relationships. First impressions are important.

The more bumps in business the bigger the potential network. Elegant symmetry.

77

IT'S NOT WHO YOU KNOW, IT'S WHO KNOWS YOU

I have spent a good deal of my life working in the media, sports and entertainment industries. I've also done a fair amount of community service work. All of these experiences have provided me with interesting people to meet, know and collaborate with. I've been very fortunate. Some of my friends are well-known. The others should be.

What surprises me is when people to go to extremes to meet celebrities or people they think will open doors for them in business. Rethinking that last sentence, I'm not so surprised that this happens – since I've done it myself, I'm embarrassed to admit. What I am disappointed with is how they do it, where they do it and when they do it. There is little regard for the privacy of the other party. The goal oftentimes is just to touch celebrity and perhaps have a story to tell friends or bragging rights on the golf course. To stretch a point, people want to be able to say that they know important people even if it is an illusion. I won't bore you with my Heidi Klum story, but I have one.

I've been around celebrities enough to know that they struggle with fulfilling the expectations of the public at these meet and greet sessions. So many of us believe that being well known and signing autographs would be fun. I can assure you that you'd grow tired of it quickly. The unfortunate part of celebrity is that it is difficult to divorce yourself from it once it occurs. I know a certain celebrity that had to wear a ski mask to go sledding with his son in a public park.

Now to the business point. There is a tendency to want to meet people that are well known or that can help you in business. People plot to make this happen. And the old adage that "It's who you know" is one of the primary drivers of this behavior.

But, who you know (at least in the context of a first meeting, a handshake, or a shared photo) is practically irrelevant. The other party has no logical reason or significant context to remember the meeting. If anything, this person is likely to purge a meeting like this from their memory because the encounters are usually so awkward to begin with. There has become a cadre of "fixers" that traffic in their supposed ability to set someone up to meet a celebrity or a business leader. This role is distained, except perhaps in the world of politics where it is tied to fundraising. Who in their right mind would consider the person who keeps foisting unwanted, awkward meetings upon them a good friend?

But we agree that knowing people is important to success. And, knowing people with access and clout can be extremely important in accelerating success. The difference is all in the phrasing.

It's not who you know (met or think you know) that is all that important. *What's important is who knows you.* It is a matter of trust and respect others have for you that makes your network of friends valuable and useful. If you know someone well, and they know you well, the foundation for mutual help and assistance is in place. This has worked well for me on all levels of business. I help lots of people – many of them referred to me by my friends. I've asked my friends for their personal help and assistance many, many times. There doesn't seem to be resentment or frustration when this happens among friends. Quite the contrary, friends are willing to help friends and welcome opportunities to do so.

So, before you start asking for autographs or favors from near-perfect strangers, ask yourself why you are doing it? What is the outcome you are looking for and how you might better achieve it? When you are building that network on the proverbial "Rolodex" ask yourself how you can get on the Rolodex of more and more people. I hope I've convinced you that it's not who you know – but who knows you, that really counts.

78

WRITE RIGHT

I have struggled with writing well my entire life. I know I'm not alone. In grade school I was always bringing home lower grades for English than for Math. This discrepancy became a characteristic that I embraced as part of my personality – that I wasn't a good writer. Looking back, the truth was much more obvious. I was lazy. The key to becoming a better writer is to write. It's a lot like golf, or the proverbial path to Carnegie Hall – practice, practice, practice.

I mention this because I discovered years ago that writing ability communicates a great deal about a person – both to themselves and more importantly to others. It is worth the effort to get your writing skills down as soon as possible. In other words, it is important to "write right."

If you find that you lack confidence with written communication, it is high time to attempt a course correction, especially if you have aspirations for a successful management or executive career. Poor writing skills eventually catch up with you. You might be able to hide for a while, but eventually you will be required to demonstrate some concise writing ability. Sometimes you are tested as a measure of competency. For young executives, improving sooner is better than delaying the inevitable.

There are two types of writing that are particularly useful in business. The first is storytelling. The ability to concisely tell a story with a memorable lesson is a skill that serves managers well. A story doesn't have to be written to be effective. But actually writing down a good story helps make it better as a listener experience when you eventually tell it. This is because the elements of good writing – a point of view, organization, clear language and expression, and a solid ending – are parts of a well-told story. One of the first things that a new person in the news media has to do is to prove that they can write stories. As an example, it is a skill in the sports business that separates the employable interns (usually the entry positions) from the "jock sniffers." The way to get good at storytelling is to: 1) do it, 2) have someone with skills and experience edit it, and then 3) do it again.

The other type of writing that is really essential in business, especially in larger corporations, is the ability to write a concise proposal. Procter & Gamble is famous for beating its new recruits into a pattern of being able to deliver a compact "one page recommendation." The theory here is that serious proposals should be able to be presented with background, a recommendation and next steps in a single page that anyone in the organization could read and comprehend. It is a lot harder to do than it is to describe. I can recall my wife working on a single document over and over to get it exactly the way her boss thought it fit the P&G mold and style. We aren't talking about the thoughtful quality of the idea or the recommendation here – those were givens. The exercise was one of expression – ultimately of writing. My wife has come to know the power of that single page memo. It has defined her as a high performer in almost everything she has attempted since.

The interesting thing is that organizations know who the good writers are. Excellent communicators can't hide their skills and they readily rise above the average. Good writers are accorded the distinction of being thought of as smarter and worthy of faster promotions.

I had the personal challenge of attempting to bring my son's writing skills up to par when he was in the sixth grade. He was a brilliant student who had natural aptitude in math and science along with the ability to read and retain facts almost at will. These were all skills that let him sail through the early primary grades. But then he hit the wall when he was forced to take a writing test. He stumbled. He was a bit embarrassed and so were we as parents. I spent a summer doing writing drills with my son every night after dinner. He hated it. But by the end of the summer we were both better writers.

Yes, it would have been more correct to have titled this chapter: "Write well." But that title would have been far less memorable. My aim is that these adages stick with you so they may be recalled with ease. "Write right" works better to accomplish this.

79

DEALING WITH THE MEDIA IS LIKE MEETING A DOBERMAN

I read once that dealing with the media is like meeting an unfamiliar Doberman for the first time. You aren't sure if they are going to lick your face or rip your throat out. It is an extreme metaphor, but one with a fundamental truth. Be careful. In fact, be very careful.

The starting point is that executives believe that media attention is guaranteed to be helpful to their business. It is like free advertising. Why pay for something that can be obtained for free? Another mistake is that executives think they are smarter than their media counterparts, and that manipulating the media is a sport they can dominate.

After working in and around the media for nearly thirty years, I have a couple of observations to share. First, reporters can be lazy. This means that sometimes they'll even eat the dog food that a company puts in front of them in an attempt to get free PR. The best way to accomplish this is to have a trusted friend of the reporter put out the dish. This saves the company from having its hand bitten. There is a role for public relations experts to make the dog food actually seem appetizing. I have enormous respect for competent and clever PR experts.

But everyone involved with the process of placing this type of story in the press, on TV or on the radio silently acknowledges that it is dog food. Fortunately, there is so much space and time to fill in these media, and so few people assigned to fill it, that the process works. We see puff pieces all the time. Sure it's dog food, but the media animal must be fed. So dog food works.

While the media is inclined to be lazy, it is likewise bred to be distrustful. They can smell really bad dog food a mile away. Serve this up at your own peril. The scent of this is an invitation to arouse the distrustful nature of the beast.

There is no better example of this than when a business has a public crisis. Serving up lies, half-truths and denials is a time-honored invitation for a reporter to become ugly and vicious. My good friend Joe Bride, a seasoned PR guy who specializes in crisis management, is adamant that the response from a company be candid, forthright and prompt. Facts and events can't be changed. But the appeal of the fare provided to the dogs can be controlled. Tell them your version of the truth. Remember, they are lazy and your version of the truth just might satisfy their appetite.

Once the media is on to a bad story provided by a bad actor they become relentless. It is instinctive. They are schooled to distrust business at all levels. They delight in creating embarrassing moments for business executives in front of the microphone or camera. You are having a very bad day if *60 Minutes* or *20/20* show up at your door uninvited, prompted by the aura of distrust. Again, reporters are under time pressures and lazy – so they dig deep where the digging is productive. Oh, I forgot to mention that they also love to win awards. Sensational stories lead to big awards and notoriety from their peers. Your goal is not to provide the big story. If the real truth limits the scope of the damage, you would be well-advised to go with the truth.

This is because there is another aspect to the media that is in play. There is so much time to fill, and lots of ways to fill it. The media consumer gets bored in a hurry. Stories have a shelf life, usually a short one. This is unless you keep extending the shelf life by providing lies that are uncovered (which almost always happens) or the person telling the story becomes a caricature. But over time even a bad story, managed well, will fade into the woodwork. This is harder to do when there is actually a legal problem. These need to be solved quickly. Providing two story cycles is just too tempting for a reporter to resist. They are able to use the same information and pictures all over again. Remember the lazy part.

The final reason that I like the title of this chapter is that it eliminates subtlety in the process of dealing with the press. A Doberman isn't subtle. They can be dangerous. Dealing with the press or the media can be equally dangerous. Be careful how you feed the dog.

WHEN WE WIN,
WE SAY NOTHING

One of my valued mentors is Charlie Mechem, who was also a close personal friend to Paul Brown, the legendary football coach. As Charlie tells it, the coach had a favorite saying which went something like this: "When we win, we say nothing. When we lose, we say even less."

In an age of braggarts and hyperbole, this is a refreshing approach to communicating operating results to the outside world. It certainly is a sound approach to dealing with the popular media. There is solid common sense behind taking this approach. Let's break it down.

From the outset, it must be acknowledged that some reporting of results is required in business. Public companies have an obligation under the law to do this. But they don't have an obligation to provide every immaterial detail or to exaggerate the future prospects of an enterprise, although they often do. The assumption is that it is important to stock valuation and the underlying cost of capital for companies to project a best-case scenario. More often than not, it is also incumbent on management to tout the prospects for future success just to keep their jobs. In summary, there is strong prejudice to paint a rosy picture – often through obfuscation of the actual truth. In doing so, there is also a tendency to heap on the verbiage – to say too much in the process. What you don't say can't get you into trouble. What you do say, can.

Internally, individuals, teams and divisions are also tempted toward the same exaggerated communication behavior. There is generally a culture of competition for recognition, promotions, personnel and other resources. The managers with a successful track record, a catchy story, or prospects for a "big win" get more attention and support. There is absolutely nothing wrong with this. If you are a manager, undoubtedly you must engage in some variation of communication that either has you evaluating performance from layers below, or reporting your performance to the next level above you. Good news finds its way up this ladder quickly. Accountability is a healthy and necessary obligation of high-performance organizations. But, that should include the bad news too.

Here's where the coach's advice comes into play. It is one thing to report and stand on a record of success – based on results. It is quite another to "spin" the communications, something I fear we have grown accustomed to hearing. Politicians can do it and get away with it because they aren't held accountable for measurable results (they can weave a vacuous story that at least half the population will swallow). It is much more difficult in business, and in sports – where there are year-end reports and scoreboards.

Great coaches, and great managers, are successful in the short term and become legendary over time. They rely on honesty and credibility to build their organizations internally and to garner the respect of the outside world.

The "greats" inherently know how to do this. If they don't naturally have the skills, they drive themselves to develop the techniques that work.

Let's go back to the coach again. What would be the point of bragging too much about a game you've already won? You won. Everybody knows it. The score is in the newspaper and on TV for everyone to see. The result is the result. This simple truth applies equally to business and sports. Bragging about it won't change the result. But it can do a couple of things that might be detrimental to the team and to your future success. First, it might unnecessarily alert the next opponent (there is always competition) to something which is working – something they need to understand to better compete against you. Second, it might lull your team into a false sense of security and dull that sense of tenacity and urgency that all healthy organizations require.

Losing is a private matter. You might not be able to say "nothing" to the outside world. But you should say about as close to nothing as is allowable and legally possible. Internally, communication can and should be much different. You never get better unless you completely understand the elements of failure, and of success. Internal examination is constantly required. Truthfulness is an absolute. "Spin" doesn't really work internally. Everybody knows the truth, and there is a tendency to discount "spin doctors" pretty quickly.

Here's one last comment on Paul Brown. The advice being proffered is from one of the most successful football coaches of all time. What you don't see behind the advice is the determination, innovation and integrity of the man that made him a success in his chosen profession. What he is really saying, without saying it, is: "Don't live in a world of self-congratulation, delusion or excuses." Get ready to play the next game.

And, there is always a next game!

ABOUT THE AUTHOR

Mark Hubbard is an independent consultant providing services exclusively to senior management, primarily in media, entertainment and sports. His areas of expertise include: business valuation, negotiating transactions, financing and restructuring, enterprise modeling, sales development and training, and executive coaching. He works with public and private companies, both in the U.S. and internationally.

Previously, Mark spent over 25 years in the broadcasting industry, from radio to television to new technologies like satellite and internet convergence. Highlights include: Senior VP, Corporate Development for Clear Channel during its major acquisition period, President of Flagship Broadcasting (TV), president of Fairmont Communications(radio), Executive VP of Osborn Communications (radio) and VP and General Manager of WKRO-FM for Taft Broadcasting. Hubbard serves as an Adjunct Professor at Renssalaer Polytechnic Institute and as Entrepreneur-in-residence at the Univesity of Notre Dame. He holds a Bachelor of Architecture degree from the University of Notre Dame and an MBA from the Wharton School,University of Pennsylvania.

Comments from expert readers...

"Business academics are usually nervous about aphorisms as a way to guide business school learning They reduce highly complex situations to simple directives, and this runs counter to the type of rigorous, thorough understanding promoted in most business classes. Not so with the aphorisms and supporting thoughts in Mark's book. I have seen him teach many students, and watched how well his ideas resonate with them and compliment their learning based on class work and prior business experience."

> —*Jeffrey Durgee, Ph.D. Associate Dean for Academic Affairs,*
> *Lally School of Management and Technology*
> *Rensselaer Polytechnic Institute*

Mark Hubbard writes with the energy and integrity of a true entrepreneur and the simplicity of a short story teller sharing with those wanting advice and willing to be mentored. He has had wide range of personal managerial and business experiences and he has known many very interesting people. His method of communicating the anecdotes of a lifetime of learning experiences is very easy to read and understand the "take aways".

> —*John Suhler, Co-founder and General Partner*
> *Veronis Suhler Stevenson, New York, NY*

Every successful executive makes management decisions based on personal experience – what works, what doesn't. Mark Hubbard delivers 80 market tested insights.

> —*Ken Roman, Retired Chairman, Author*
> *Ogilvy & Mather, New York, NY*

Hubbard provides insights gathered from a lifetime in business and observing business. He has seen well crafted strategies paired with flawed tactics, or the other way around, each born in fundamental principles, some right, some gone wrong. It is an excellent overlay of common sense easily applicable to everyday business situations.

> —*John Dille, President, CEO*
> *Federated Media, Elkhart, IN*